STORIES FROM
EARLY ISLAM

by

Rashid Ahmad Chaudhry

Stories From Early Islam

by

Rashid Ahmad Chaudhry

ISLAM INTERNATIONAL PUBLICATIONS LTD.

Stories From Early Islam
Revised edition of the book *Golden Deeds of Muslims*
Written by Rashid Ahmad Chaudhry

First edition published in UK, 1975
Second edition: 1989
Third edition: 1990 (Pbk)
British Library Cataloguing in Publication Data
Title: Stories from early Islam (Golden deeds of Muslims)
Author: Rashid Ahmad Chaudhri, 1934-
Subjects: Juvenile literature; Islamic stories: 297
Identifier: ISBN 9781853723575 (pbk.); ISBN 1853723576 (pbk.);
ISBN 185372291X (pbk.);
BNB GBB105256; System number 015475302
Shelfmark(s): General Reference Collection YK.2010.a.34214;
UIN: BLL01015475302

Fourth edition published in India, 2017
Reprinted in the UK, 2017
© Islam International Publications Ltd.

Published by
Islam International Publications Ltd.
Islamabad, Sheephatch Lane
Tilford, Surrey GU10 2AQ, UK

Printed in UK at
Raqeem Press
Tilford, Surrey
For further information please visit www.alislam.org.

ISBN 978-1-84880-890-4
10 9 8 7 6 5

CONTENTS

Foreword .... *v*
Foreword to the Present Edition .... *vii*

Stories from Early Islam 1
The Religion of Islam 3
Islamic Worship 21
The Word of God 33
The Prophet's Personality and Character 43
The Wisdom of the Holy Prophet 49
Slaves Get their Freedom 55
Umar Accepts Islam 59
I will Stand by You 65
The Journey to Ta'if 69
Fear Not, God is with Us 75
The Prophecy about the Gold Bangles 83
Two Young Eagles 87
The Undecided Battle 93
A Strange Contest 101
Two Martyrs 105
Sword of Allah 111
The Spirit of Sacrifice 117
Who can Save You Now? 121
Feeding the Guest in Darkness 125
Equal Justice 129

Non-discrimination 133
The Poisoned Meat 137
Feeding a Large Company 143
A Loving Recompense 147
Kindness towards Parents 151
Letters to Kings 155
Power of Prayer 161
Umar in Disguise 165
Preferring Others to Oneself 171
Victorious Return to Makkah 177
Islam on the March 187

Publisher's Note *195*

FOREWORD

Mr. Rashid Ahmad obtained his Master's degree in Islamic Studies and subsequently his L.L.B. and B.T. at Punjab University, Pakistan. He is at present a teacher in one of the Comprehensive schools in London. In this book, he combines his knowledge of the subject with nineteen years of teaching experience to produce a collection of stories about famous Muslims, supplementing such stories with a brief introduction about Islam.

The stories make compelling reading matter for both young and old. They give an insight to the simple lives led by the early Muslims and show how such people sacrificed their lives, property and honour for the sake of their faith and thus became popularly known as martyrs or heroes. The reader has been

saved the trouble of sifting facts from myths in order to present the truth in its barest form: these are true stories.

All true stories have a moral and the collection in this book are no exception. We learn how the companions of the Holy Prophet Muhammad, peace and blessings of Allah be upon him, underwent various trials and how a firm belief in the powers of the Almighty helped them overcome the enemies.

Children will welcome this book and will want to read it again and again. They love stories as they present a logical sequence of events, providing an accurate description of various characters and inspire them to model themselves along the footsteps of a famous hero. All parents are urged to encourage this experience in order to mould the character of the present generation who have a tremendous lot to learn from the past and upon whom we have high hopes for the future.

Indeed this is a most useful book to have in any library.

B. A. Rafiq
Imam
The London Mosque
February 1975

FOREWORD
TO THE PRESENT EDITION

The book *Stories from Early Islam* was first printed in 1975 under the title *Golden Deeds of Muslims*. This was a collection of inspiring incidents from Islamic history intended to teach our youth of the lofty principles and morals of Islam. Since its first publication, we have received a large number of requests for this book from the United Kingdom and abroad.

The Children's Book Committee, under the guidance and supervision of Hazrat Khalifatul-Masih IV[rta] had revised the text and added a few illustrations, which we hope will be welcomed by children, parents, and teachers. We are especially grateful to our late brother, Dawood Summers, for his many helpful ideas and comments.

Per the instructions of Hazrat Khalifatul-Masih V[aba], we have redesigned the format in this present edition, added further illustrations, and revised spellings of Arabic words to help children pronounce them more accurately. Readers are urged to invoke blessings on the Holy Prophet Muhammad whenever his name appears by saying, 'may peace and blessings of Allah be upon him', and recite 'may Allah be pleased with him/her' when the name of one of his Companions is mentioned.

We would like to express our gratitude to Waseem Ahmad Sayed, Syed Faraz Hussain, and Abdul-Wahab Mirza for the

individual contributions they made to this current edition. May Allah, the Benevolent Lord, bestow His blessings upon each and every individual who contributed to this booklet and its earlier editions, and inspire its readers to uphold the high standards that Islam demands. *Aameen.*

Al-Haaj Munir-ud-Din Shams
Additional Wakeel-ut-Tasneef, London
January, 2017

STORIES FROM EARLY ISLAM

THE RELIGION OF ISLAM

The religion preached and practised by the Prophet Muhammad, may peace and blessings of Allah be upon him, is known as Islam. The name 'Islam' was given to this religion by God Himself. We read in the Holy Qur'an:

> This day, I have perfected for you, your religion, and completed My favour on you and chosen for you Islam as a religion. (Holy Quran 5:4)

There is no other religion which can claim that its name was given by God. The above verse also tells us that Islam is a perfect religion.

'Islam' is an Arabic word which means 'peace'. It also means complete submission, i.e. complete submission to the Will of God. Therefore peace with God, peace with fellow-beings, and submission to God, is the essence of Islam.

Those who accept Islam as their faith are Muslims, which would mean peaceful and submissive people. A Muslim, therefore, in submission to the Will of God, has to devote his life in establishing peace on earth. A Muslim believes in:

- One God,
- The Angels,
- The Books of God,
- The Prophets, and Life after Death.
- Belief or faith is called *Iman*. One who believes is therefore a *mo'min* (believer). The words Muslim and *mo'min* convey the same meaning.

Islam is a great bounty of God. It is a blessing not only for Muslims but also for the whole of mankind. It safeguards people against all social evils.

Drugs, liquor and all other intoxicants are totally forbidden in Islam. Gambling is not allowed. Eating of the flesh of swine is not permitted. All these are harmful to us and to society. The lending of money on interest is also forbidden as it tends to accumulate wealth within a limited circle and is otherwise harmful in its effects.

Islamic doctrine has five aspects which are known as the five pillars of Islam. They are as follows:

1. **Kalimah**—To bear witness that God is one and Muhammad is His Messenger.
2. **Salat**—To say five daily prayers at their appointed times.
3. **Saum**—To observe fasts during the month of Ramadan.
4. **Zakat**—To contribute a certain percentage of wealth for charity and other noble causes, mentioned in the Holy Qur'an.
5. **Hajj**—To go for pilgrimage to Makkah at least once in one's life-time if physically and financially possible, during the Hajj season.

Study Questions

QUESTION 1: What is the name of the religion preached by the Prophet Muhammad, may peace and blessings of Allah be upon him?

YOUR RESPONSE: _____

_____

_____

QUESTION 2: Who gave the name to this religion?

YOUR RESPONSE: _____

_____

_____

QUESTION 3: What does the word 'Muslim' mean?

YOUR RESPONSE: _____

_____

QUESTION 4: Name the five pillars of Islam and explain each one of them.

YOUR RESPONSE:

THE HOLY PROPHET

May peace and blessings of Allah be upon him

When people drift away from the true path, which leads to God and turn their backs on Divine guidance, a Prophet is sent by Almighty God to bring them close to Him again. This was the case with the Holy Prophet Muhammad. Before his advent, almost all the Arabs were idol worshippers. It was said that there were three hundred and sixty idols in the Ka'abah alone. The rest of the world was in no better shape. The prevalent faiths had entered upon a period of decay and their followers exhibited none of the virtues taught to them. In Arabia, drinking and gambling were common practices. Women in Arab society had neither status nor rights. Burying of female children alive was

practised among some families. It was among such people that the Holy Prophet of Islam was born.

He was born at Makkah in Arabia in 570 A.D. Makkah was a trading centre where caravans stopped on their way from Syria to Yemen and to the far east. It was also regarded as a holy place because of the Ka'abah. The Ka'abah, according to the Holy Qur'an, is the first House of worship that was built for mankind. People from all parts of Arabia used to come to Makkah to pay a visit to this House. There was also a holy well called 'Zamzam' close to the Ka'abah.

The Holy Prophet Muhammad belonged to a noble family of Arabia called the Quraish. His father's name was Abdullah and his mother's Amina. His father died a few months before the child was born and his mother died when he was six. He was left in the care of his grandfather, Abdul Mutalib. Two years later his grandfather also died. Thereafter, he was brought up by his uncle Abu Taalib.

Trade was the main occupation of the people of Makkah in those days. When Muhammad grew up, he was employed by Khadijah, a rich widow of Makkah, as her trade agent. She was very impressed by his honesty and offered him her hand in marriage. Khadijah at the time of marriage was forty years old, while he was only twenty-five.

TRADE CARAVAN

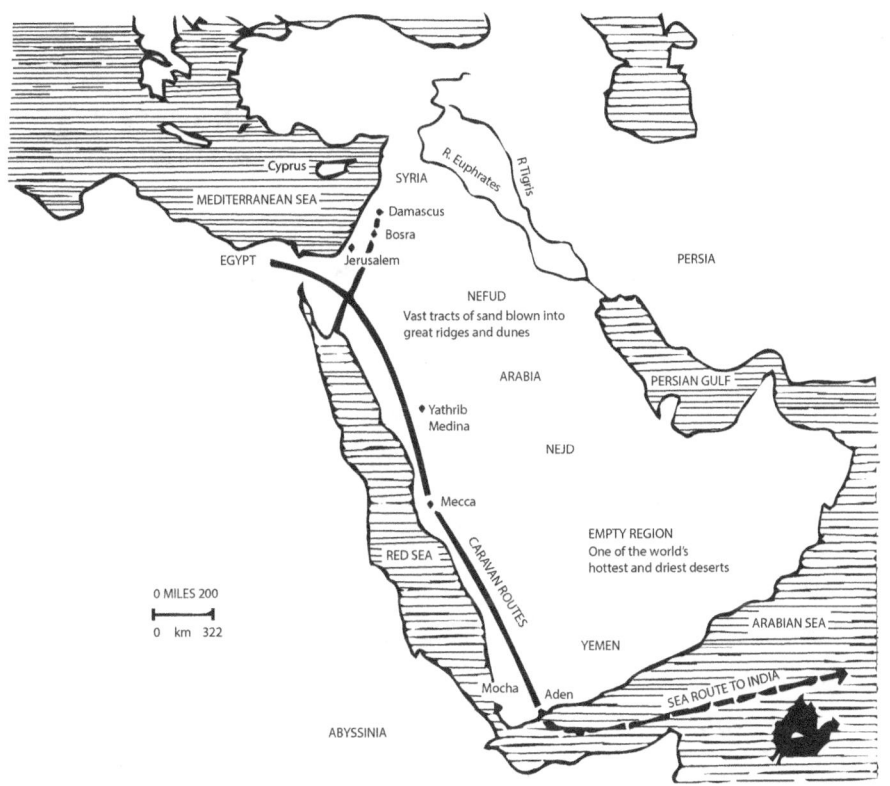

ARABIAN TRADE ROUTE

From his childhood, Muhammad was content, quiet and given to reflection and meditation. He took no part in quarrels and rivalries, rather he tried to put an end to them. He was pious, truthful and honest so much so that he was given the titles of *As-Siddeeq* 'the truthful one' and *Al-Ameen,* 'the trusted one', by the people. As he grew up, he was greatly concerned about the vices and ills of the society in which he lived. He loved solitude and used to retire for meditation to a hollow in the mountain called Hira, a few miles out of Makkah. At the age of forty he received a revelation from God that he had been appointed a Prophet whose duty it was to reform mankind. One day when he was meditating in the hollow, he heard a voice commanding him to recite. He was much perturbed. He replied that he did not know how to recite. The voice insisted and so Muhammad began to recite as he was instructed. Revelation was a new experience for him. He was full of anxiety because of the responsibility which God was about to place on him. He went home

THE CAVE OF HIRA

immediately and related the incident to his wife Khadijah. She said to him:

> You are kind and considerate to your relations. You help the poor and bear their burden. You try to restore the virtues that have disappeared. You honour the guests and help those who are in difficulty. Surely God will never let you fail.

She suggested that they should go to her cousin Waraqa bin Naufal, a Christian hermit and consult him.

Waraqa heard the account that Muhammad gave him and said:

> I am sure the angel that descended on Moses had descended on you. I wish I would be alive to give you my support when your people will turn you out.

'Will they turn me out?' asked the Prophet in surprise. The Christian hermit said: 'Never has that, which has come to you, come to anyone without his people turning against him.'

When the Holy Prophet started his Divine mission, he was opposed by all except a few. The majority of the people rejected him and ridiculed him. Every effort was made to stop the message of Islam. He and his followers were persecuted, so much so that they had to leave Makkah and migrate to a town called Yathrib, about two hundred miles north of Makkah. The people of Yathrib accepted Islam in large numbers and so it became

the first Muslim city and was thereafter known as Madinatun-Nabi (Madinah for short), meaning the city of the Prophet.

When Makkans saw that Islam was prospering in Madinah, they decided to destroy it by force. They attacked the city several times, but were defeated each time. These hostilities extended over several years. At last a truce was agreed upon and a treaty was signed by the Muslims and the Makkans at a place called Hudaibiyyah. Within two years the Makkans broke the treaty. The Holy Prophet was therefore forced to march upon Makkah. With ten thousand of his followers he went to Makkah. The helpless Makkans surrendered and he entered the city victorious.

During the life-time of the Holy Prophet, Islam had spread throughout Arabia. He died at Madinah at the age of 63, and was buried there.

Study Questions

QUESTION 1: Where was Muhammad, may peace and blessings of Allah be upon him, born?

YOUR RESPONSE:

QUESTION 2: Why was Makkah regarded as a holy place?

YOUR RESPONSE:

QUESTION 3: Who took care of Muhammad when his mother died?

YOUR RESPONSE: _____

_____

QUESTION 4: What was the chief occupation of Meccans in those days?

YOUR RESPONSE: _____

_____

_____

QUESTION 5: What was the name of the mountain to which Muhammad used to retire for meditation?

YOUR RESPONSE: _____

_____

_____

QUESTION 6: How far is Madinah from Makkah?

YOUR RESPONSE:

QUESTION 7: Who was Waraqa bin Naufal? What did he say in reply when Muhammad related his experience to him?

YOUR RESPONSE:

ISLAMIC WORSHIP

Islam lays great stress upon Divine worship. Indeed it is regarded as the purpose of man's creation. The object of worship is to strengthen man's relationship with God. In the Holy Qur'an God says:

> Call on Me, I will respond to you. (Holy Quran 40:61)

In the Islamic form of worship, an intermediary is not needed. A man prays to God and seeks to establish relationship with Him. He prays with a firm belief that no sincere prayer is in vain. In Islam, it is a great sin to worship any other besides God. Allah alone has the power to answer prayers, so we should ask each and every thing from Him.

Islamic worship may be divided into two categories:

1. Formal worship such as Prayer Services, Pilgrimage to the House of Allah (Hajj), Fasting and Zakat. Prayer service means worship in congregation.
2. Informal worship such as remembrance of God, called 'Dhikr'.

Islam prescribes five daily Prayers called *Salat* at appointed times. They are as follows:

- **Fajr Prayer**..............................Before Sunrise
- **Zuhr Prayer**.....................................At Noon
- (when the sun begins to decline)
- **Asr Prayer**............................In the Afternoon
- **Maghrib Prayer**..............shortly after Sunset
- **Isha Prayer**..............................In the Evening

The Islamic Prayer is quite different from those pre-scribed in other religions. It has both an individual and a collective part. All Prayer services are led by an Imam. There is no Priesthood in Islam. Any person who has some religious knowledge can lead the Prayer service. Generally, he is chosen for his piety and learning. If there are only two Muslims, one of them leads the Prayer. A man can lead the Prayer in his house with members of his family following him, but if a person is alone and can find no one with whom he can join in Prayer, he shall perform it by himself.

On Fridays there is a special service called *Salatul-Jumu'ah*, which is performed in place of the Zuhr Prayer. In this service the Imam delivers a sermon before the Prayer. Although a Muslim may offer his Prayers anywhere, in home, in the open, or even on board a ship or train, he should try to offer them as a member of the congregation in a mosque.

Before each Prayer, Adhan (Call to Prayer) is called. The one who calls out the Adhan is called a 'Muadhdhin'. He stands on a raised platform or in a minaret, with his face towards the Ka'abah and makes the announcement, the translation of which is as follows:

> Allah is the Greatest; Allah is the Greatest
> Allah is the Greatest; Allah is the Greatest
> I bear witness that there is none worthy of worship except Allah
> I bear witness that there is none worthy of worship except Allah
> I bear witness that Muhammad is the Messenger of Allah
> I bear witness that Muhammad is the Messenger of Allah
> Come to Prayer; Come to Prayer
> Come to Success; Come to Success
> Allah is the Greatest; Allah is the Greatest
> There is none worthy of worship except Allah'.

A BOY SAYING ADHAN

On hearing this call, a Muslim leaves his work and comes to the mosque. He performs ablution i.e. washes his face, hands and feet in the prescribed manner.

There are no seats or places reserved for anybody in a mosque. The Imam stands in front of the congregation with his face towards the Ka'abah. Behind him people stand in rows facing the same direction. In the house of Allah all are equal regardless of rank, office, colour or race. These gatherings are not mixed. Women stand separately from men. Everyone follows the Imam as he goes through various postures. The different postures are standing, bowing, prostration and sitting.

The Muslims gather for Divine worship in the simplest possible manner. No music, choir, or congregational singing is permitted in the Prayers. Conversation is totally prohibited. There are no images, pictures or paintings in a mosque. All these are prohibited because they distract the attention of a worshipper.

In addition to the prescribed Services, Muslims offer prayers and devote themselves silently to the remembrance of

God during the course of the day, even when their hands may be otherwise occupied, or when walking or riding.

Fasting is another form of worship. A Fast means abstention from food and drink from dawn to sunset for the pleasure of God. The Islamic Fast is different from the Fasts prescribed in other religions. For example, Hindus and Christians are permitted to eat certain kinds of food during the period of their Fasts, while a Muslim does not eat or drink anything from dawn to sunset. This goes on for twenty nine or thirty days, throughout Ramadan, the month in which the Qur'an was first revealed to the Holy Prophet.

Another form of worship is known as Zakat. It is a kind of religious tax imposed on certain types of possession and wealth. Muslims who possess for one complete year, cash or goods, beyond a minimum, pay Zakat according to a specified rate, which on the average, works out at 2 1/2% of the capital value of the form of wealth on which it is assessed. The proceeds of Zakat are distributed among the poorer sections of the community, and other noble causes mentioned in the Holy Qur'an.

Hajj or the Pilgrimage to Makkah is another form of Islamic worship. It is obligatory upon all Muslims who can afford the journey to perform Hajj at least once in their life-time. Millions of Muslims from all parts of the world gather at Makkah to perform this worship every year, during the prescribed days.

There are two Muslim festivals. One is called 'Eid-ul-Fitr', a festival at the end of the month of Fasting. Congregational

AN ARTIST'S IMPRESSION OF THE HOLY PLACES

Services are held at convenient places where large numbers gather for the worship, and the Imam delivers a sermon.

The second festival is called *Eid-ul-Ad'ha,* the festival of sacrifice. It is celebrated in memory of the readiness of Ibrahim [Abraham] to sacrifice his only son Ismail [Ishmael], as he considered God had commanded him to do. An extra Service is held in the forenoon in which a sermon is delivered. On this day those Muslims who can afford to slaughter an animal, do so after the Prayer, as a sacrifice.

The person who offers the sacrifice is allowed to use a portion of the meat, the remainder is distributed among the relatives, friends, neighbours and the poor. Millions of animals are slaughtered all over the world on this occasion.

Study Questions

QUESTION 1 What is meant by *Salat* (Prayer Service)?

YOUR RESPONSE:

QUESTION 2 How many Prayer Services are prescribed for a Muslim daily? Give their names and timings.

YOUR RESPONSE:

QUESTION 3: What is meant by the following:

ZAKAT: _____

_____

MUADHDHIN: _____

_____

ADHAN: _____

_____

IMAM: _____

_____

QUESTION 4: Where may a Muslim offer his Prayers?

YOUR RESPONSE: _____

_____

QUESTION 5: What according to Islam is the purpose of man's creation?

YOUR RESPONSE: _____

QUESTION 6: Towards which direction do Muslims face during a Prayer Service?

YOUR RESPONSE: _____

QUESTION 7 Where do Muslims go to perform Hajj?

YOUR RESPONSE: _____

QUESTION 8: On what occasion does the Imam deliver a sermon?

YOUR RESPONSE: _____

QUESTION 9: Name the two Muslim festivals and give their background.

YOUR RESPONSE: _____

CALLIGRAPHY IN A DECORATED QUR'AN

THE WORD OF GOD

The word 'Qur'an' literally means that which is recited, announced or proclaimed. It is the collection of the verbal revelations bestowed upon the Prophet[saw] during a period of about 23 years and is the actual word of God. The first revelation comprising only a few verses, was revealed to the Holy Prophet[saw] on the mountain of Hira. Thereafter, revelation continued until his death. Whenever any portion of the Qur'an was revealed to him, he committed it to memory. Many of his followers did the same as they heard it. Some of them even wrote the verses on anything available like pieces of leather, bark of trees or stones. In order to safeguard it, the Prophet[saw] had also appointed several persons who recorded it in writing whenever a revelation was received.

The Holy Qur'an is the book most often recited and quoted throughout the world. It is obligatory for every Muslim to participate in five Prayer Services during the day. The greater part of these Prayers is composed of portions of the Holy Qur'an. Thus a Muslim recites a portion of the Holy Book every day. In addition most of them start their day with a recitation from it.

During the time of Abu Bakr, the first *Khalifah,* it was decided to collect the whole Qur'an in one volume. Zaid bin Thabit, a prominent Companion of the Holy Prophet[saw] was appointed for this purpose. He took great care to compile it in the form of a book, the sequence of which was laid down by the Holy Prophet[saw] himself.

During the time of the third *Khalifah,* Uthman, an official version of the Holy Qur'an was issued. Seven copies were made, which were then sent to different parts of the Muslim world. These seven became the standard texts from which other copies were made.

All Muslims learn to read the Holy Qur'an in Arabic, even though that may not be their own language. Almost every Muslim knows some chapters of the Book by heart and in each generation there are hundreds of thousands of people who can recite the whole Book from beginning to end from their memory.

The Holy Qur'an has been translated into all the major languages of the world and the work continues to be carried on. The Qur'an has 114 chapters, called *Suras.* Each chapter, except

READING THE HOLY QUR'AN

the ninth begins with the invocation 'In the name of Allah, Most Gracious, Ever Merciful'.

The Holy Qur'an is the only book in the world which claims that every word contained in it is the actual word of God, and that He has taken upon Himself the responsibility of preserving the purity of the text in all ages. This has been demonstrated throughout history. The text of the Qur'an has continued without any alteration or modification.

A Muslim has to believe not only in the Qur'an but also in all the Books sent by God to previous Prophets from time to time. Unfortunately none of the previous Books retained its original text intact.

In the Holy Qur'an, mention has been made of Adam, Abraham, Joseph, David, Solomon, Jesus and several other Biblical Prophets (peace be upon them all). They are honoured as true Messengers of God. Mary, the mother of Jesus, is described as a model of righteousness. According to the Holy

Qur'an, Jesus was a Prophet of God, and not a Divine being as believed by Christians.

The Holy Qur'an condemns the notion of the Trinity and the association of anything or any one else, with God as His partner. It teaches that there is only one God, whose proper name is Allah, and that the worst sin is to associate any other being with Him.

The Holy Qur'an stresses the equality of mankind. It recognises the divisions between people into tribes and sub-tribes, but explains that these divisions are meant for identification only. The only badge of honour is a person's righteousness. It lays down that no nation, tribe or race is superior to others.

The Holy Qur'an teaches that worship does not merely mean that a man should concentrate upon and offer homage to God but also consists in serving fellow human beings.

It seeks to bring about an equitable adjustment in the distribution of wealth through Zakat, alms and charity.

It determines the duties and rights of the State and its

members. It discusses in detail the code of conduct in times of war and peace, as well as international relations and treaties.

It teaches man to lead a simple life, to be honest, kind and truthful in his dealing with others. It prohibits anything that has a tendency to incite people to foolish and irresponsible behaviour. Hence it puts a ban on all intoxicants and gambling, etc.

The Holy Qur'an absolutely refutes the theory of hereditary sin, put forward by Christianity. It says that every child is sinless when it is born.

The Holy Qur'an contains several prophecies relating to later times, some of which have already been fulfilled. For example, it prophesied about the time when quicker means of transport would be used. It also mentioned about the extension of the earth, a prophecy which was fulfilled in a way when man set his foot on the moon. It claims that all heavenly bodies revolve in different orbits.

Another prophecy contained in the Holy Qur'an is about Pharoah. It was revealed that when Pharoah was drowned, his body was saved and was preserved so that it should serve as a sign for future generations. This incident is mentioned only in the Holy Qur'an. The Bible and other authentic records of that time are silent about this.

The prophecy came true in this century when the body of the Pharoah was discovered and identified. This established the fact that after he was drowned, his dead body was recovered, embalmed and preserved.

The Holy Qur'an provides a solution for every problem of the world. It is a Book of guidance for the people of all ages.

Study Questions

QUESTION 1: How was the text of the Holy Qur'an preserved?

YOUR RESPONSE:

QUESTION 2: How does the Qur'an differ from the previous Scriptures?

YOUR RESPONSE:

QUESTION 3: How many chapters are there in the Holy Qur'an?

YOUR RESPONSE: _____

QUESTION 4: What status does the Qur'an give to Jesus?

YOUR RESPONSE: _____

QUESTION 5: What, according to the Holy Qur'an is the worst sin?

YOUR RESPONSE: _____

_____

_____

QUESTION 6: Mention some of the teachings of the Holy Qur'an?

YOUR RESPONSE:

QUESTION 7: Mention some of the prophecies contained in the Holy Qur'an.

YOUR RESPONSE:

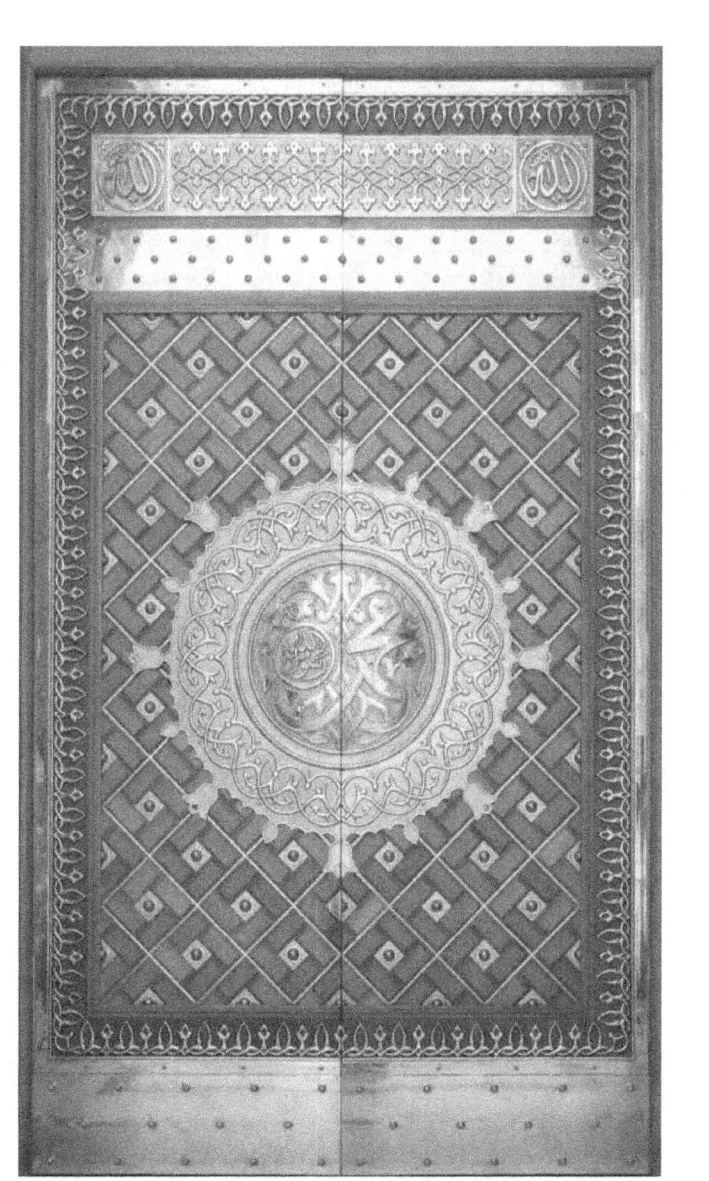

THE PROPHET'S PERSONALITY AND CHARACTER

The life of no other religious Teacher or Prophet is so well recorded as the life of the Prophet of Islam. Soon after his death, his followers began to collect the sayings or statements made by or about the Prophet. A detailed account of his life has thus been handed down to us, so that we have a complete picture of every aspect of his life. Such was the love and devotion that the Messenger of Allah inspired in the minds and hearts of his followers that they eagerly watched his every movement and gesture, and paid great attention to every word and phrase he uttered. The faithful transmission of all that the beloved Prophet had said and the detailed description of all that he did and the manner of his doing it, became a most praise-worthy practice, and soon there developed a whole science of Tradition. From these Traditions, a modest attempt is made here to draw a pen picture of the Prophet, as he appeared to those among whom he moved as an intimate, affectionate companion, counsellor, comrade and friend. Let us see what sort of man he really was.

We know what he looked like. He was a man of medium height, well built. His hair was black, and a bit curly. His complexion was fair and bright. He had a broad forehead. His beard was full. He walked briskly bending forward slightly.

He spoke clearly and deliberately, so that those present could follow him easily and remember what he said. He used to repeat three times to ensure that his meaning was fully grasped.

He treated all very kindly. He was particularly good with children. He shared in people's joys and griefs. He was truthful, gentle and courteous. He was extremely simple in matters of food and drink. He never drank wine, but liked a cup of milk. He liked honey with barley bread. He usually had a modest meal, consisting of a handful of dates.

His clothes were simple and had many patches on them. He despised the pomp of royalty. When he had become the ruler of Madinah, his life was much the same. He used to mend his shoes and clothes himself. The only luxury he allowed himself was perfume, which he loved very much. He loved cleanliness and had inculcated this habit in his followers as well.

The Holy Prophet of Islam was exceptionally kind to animals. On one occasion he saw a donkey which had been branded on the face. He inquired the reason for this and was

told that it was done for the purpose of identifying well-bred animals. He was very displeased and forbade the branding of animals on the face, as it is a very sensitive part of the body. He said that in future, animals should be branded on their legs, if it had to be done, at all.

On another occasion he saw somebody who had caught the young ones of a dove. He told him to set them free and not to torture the mother.

Another thing of great importance which the Holy Prophet taught to the people was to work with their own hands. He himself set the example, by helping his wives in their household duties. He milked his own goats. He carried stones when the mosque at Madinah was built. No work was beneath his dignity.

He looked upon this world as a place in which one lives as a wayfarer. He said, 'My case is like that of a traveller who stops at noon under the shade of a tree to rest for a while, before going

further on his journey'. He did not desire worldly riches and comforts.

He listened to everybody with patience. If a person treated him rudely he never attempted retaliation. He was ever ready to forgive people their faults and trespasses. His generosity towards his enemies has no parallel in the history of the world. When Makkah fell to Muslims and the Holy Prophet entered the city victorious, those who had treated him and his followers most cruelly received his free pardon even without asking for it. Thirteen years of persecution were forgiven and forgotten in one single moment.

He always treated his neighbours with extreme kindness and consideration. He used to say that the angel Gabriel has emphasized consideration towards one's neighbour so often that he sometimes began to think that a neighbour would perhaps be included among the prescribed heirs.

He devoted most of his time to the worship of God. Sometimes he stood so long in Prayer that his feet would be swollen.

In fact in the words of Aishah, the wife of the Holy Prophet, his character was the Qur'an.

Study Questions

QUESTION 1: What is meant by 'Traditions'?

YOUR RESPONSE:

QUESTION 2: Write a brief essay on the character of the Prophet of Islam.

YOUR RESPONSE:

THE HOLY PROPHET'S MOSQUE

THE WISDOM OF THE HOLY PROPHET

May peace and blessings of Allah be upon him

The Ka'abah is the first House of worship that was built for mankind for the worship of one True God. We cannot say who built it, but we are told by God in the Holy Qur'an that it was rebuilt by Ibrahim and his son Ismail. The Ka'abah has been the centre of life in Makkah from the time it was rebuilt. People from far and wide came here for the pilgrimage to the House of Allah. In the days of the Holy Prophet Muhammad, all the important decisions about the affairs of the city were made at

the Ka'abah. Whenever any dispute arose, the heads of the various families living in Makkah would gather there to discuss it.

Sometime after the birth of the Holy Prophet of Islam, the Ka'abah was in a very bad state of repairs and the people of Makkah had decided to rebuild it. A dispute arose about the placing of the famous Black Stone. The Black Stone has always been held in reverence because it was the Prophet Ibrahim who placed it in the Ka'abah. It is a stone in the south eastern corner of the wall and is about four feet from the ground.

Several leading families of the Quraish tribe claimed the honour of placing the stone in position. The controversy became heated, tempers rose and threats were exchanged. Some of the leaders sensed the delicate situation and feared that it might lead to violence if no agreement was reached. So one of them suggested that the matter should be settled by the one who would be the first to arrive at the Ka'abah. Muhammad chanced to enter the enclosure of the Ka'abah at that moment, so the dispute was referred to him.

Muhammad listened very calmly to the claims of each party. He spread out his cloak on the ground and placed the Black Stone on it. He then invited the leaders of all the tribes to lift the cloak and carry it to the place, where it had to be put in position. When the stone was thus carried to the place, he lifted it and placed it in the wall. This satisfied everybody, as each leader had been given the honour of lifting the sacred stone. Thus a dispute which had threatened bloodshed was resolved peacefully, through the wisdom of the Holy Prophet of Islam.

THE HOLY KAʿBAH

Study Questions

QUESTION 1: Who built the Ka'abah?

YOUR RESPONSE: _____

_____

QUESTION 2: Why was the Ka'abah the centre of life for Makkah?

YOUR RESPONSE: _____

_____

_____

QUESTION 3: Why could the people of Makkah not decide about placing the Black Stone in position?

YOUR RESPONSE:

QUESTION 4: How was the dispute resolved?

YOUR RESPONSE:

SLAVES GET THEIR FREEDOM

Long ago, people used to buy and sell men and women. Even children were bought and sold in the open market. They were called slaves and they used to work for their masters throughout their lives. Islam was the first religion to denounce slavery. The Holy Prophet of Islam and his Companions always tried to buy slaves and free them. Here is the story of one such slave whose name was Zaid.

Zaid belonged to a noble family and was an intelligent young man. He was captured while in his teens in a tribal raid, and was sold from one person to another, until finally he was purchased by Khadijah, a rich lady of Makkah. When Muhammad married Khadijah, she offered all her belongings including her slaves to him. He set all the slaves free, but Zaid begged him to let him continue to live with him. So Zaid remained with Muhammad and with time his attachment to him grew.

It so happened that the father and an uncle of Zaid traced him to Makkah. They came to Muhammad and asked that he should be allowed to return with them. They offered to pay as much ransom as might be demanded. Muhammad told them that Zaid was free and that he could go wherever he liked. He sent for Zaid and showed him his father and uncle. Zaid was much pleased to see them after such a long time. He was told that his mother had remained grief-stricken all through the period of separation and was waiting eagerly for his return. They

then asked him to accompany them home but Zaid refused to go. He said, 'Father, is there any person in the world who does not love his parents? My heart is full of love for you and my mother. But I love this man Muhammad so much that I cannot endure separation from him.'

Both Zaid's father and his uncle tried to persuade him to return home but failed. He remained firm in his decision not to leave his gracious master, though he sent loving messages to his mother. When Muhammad saw his devotion, he took him to the Ka'abah, and in the presence of his father and uncle declared that Zaid would henceforth be his son.

Study Questions

QUESTION 1: Who was Zaid?

YOUR RESPONSE: _____

QUESTION 2: Who came to Makkah to take Zaid away?

YOUR RESPONSE:

QUESTION 3: Why did Zaid refuse to go home?

YOUR RESPONSE:

QUESTION 4: What was the announcement made in the Ka'abah by the Holy Prophet?

YOUR RESPONSE:

UMAR ACCEPTS ISLAM

Before accepting Islam, Umar was one of the worst enemies of the Muslims. He was a great soldier. When he saw that in spite of the strong opposition, Islam was spreading day by day, he decided to kill the Prophet[saw] in order to finish the new Faith for ever. With this vicious motive, he took a sword in hand and set out in search of the Holy Prophet[saw]. A friend met him on the way and asked him where he was going. 'To kill Muhammad', replied Umar. 'But don't you know that your sister Faatimah and her husband have already become Muslims' said the man. Umar was greatly shocked to learn this. He decided to deal with them first before going to the Prophet[saw].

As he reached his sister's house, he heard a recitation being made inside the house. A Muslim teacher, Khabbaab by name was teaching them the Holy Book. As soon as they saw Umar approaching, Khabbaab hid himself, and Faatimah hid the leaves on which the verses were written.

Umar faced his sister and brother-in-law and said, 'I learnt that you have joined the new religion which Muhammad has brought.'

They tried to explain to him, to calm him down, but Umar was in no mood to listen to any explanation. He raised his sword to hit his brother-in-law. Faatimah, who was standing nearby, stepped in quickly to save her husband, and was injured slightly in doing so. Blood began to flow from her face. She

looked straight into Umar's eyes and said bravely 'Yes, we are Muslims now and shall remain so. Do what you may'.

Seeing the blood on his sister's face and hearing this bold reply, Umar calmed down quickly. Soon he was a changed man. He requested that the leaves of the Holy Qur'an, which were being read, be shown to him. Faatimah refused lest he should destroy them. Umar promised that he would not do so. She told him to wash himself, and when he did, Faatimah gave him the leaves. Very calmly he began to read the verses of the Holy Qur'an, and in no time the truth dawned on him. He decided to become a Muslim. In the meantime Khabbaab had come out of his hiding. He said 'God is my witness, only yesterday, I heard the Prophet[saw] pray for the conversion of Umar or Amr bin Hisham. Your change is the result of that prayer'.

Umar asked them where the Prophet[saw] was and made straight for the place, still carrying his sword in his hand. When he reached the house, where the Holy Prophet[saw] was sitting with some of his Companions, he knocked at the door. The

Companions peeped through the keyhole and saw him standing with sword in hand. They hesitated to open the door. The Holy Prophet[saw] told them to open the door. Umar came in. The Prophet[saw] asked him 'Umar, what brings you here?' 'I have come to accept Islam', said Umar.

The Holy Prophet[saw] and the Companions were much pleased to hear this and all of them said with one voice 'Allah-o-Akbar', Allah is the Greatest. The news spread throughout Makkah. It was a severe blow to the enemies of Islam, as Umar was a very brave and influential man in Makkah.

The Muslims up to that time used to say their Prayers secretly behind closed doors. Now as Umar was one of them, they decided to say their Prayers openly. Umar had done so much for Islam, that after the death of the first *Khalifah,* Abu Bakr, he was chosen as *Khalifah* by the Muslims.

Study Questions

QUESTION 1: Who was Umar?

YOUR RESPONSE: _____

_____

QUESTION 2: What was in his mind when he was going to the Prophet^{saw}?

YOUR RESPONSE: _____

_____

_____

_____

QUESTION 3: What did his friend say to him?

YOUR RESPONSE: _____

_____

_____

QUESTION 4: What was the name of Umar's sister?

YOUR RESPONSE:

QUESTION 5: What made Umar a changed person?

YOUR RESPONSE:

QUESTION 6: Why were the Companions reluctant to open the door?

YOUR RESPONSE:

QUESTION 7: How did the Muslims of Makkah receive the news of Umar's conversion?

YOUR RESPONSE:

I WILL STAND BY YOU

The religion of Islam made a strong appeal to the weak and the oppressed. The slaves who suffered great hardships, began to hope that the message of Islam might bring an end to slavery. Women, who were treated worse than animals, began to feel that the time might come when they would be given the rights due to them in the society. So a large number of the early converts came from such groups.

As the number of Muslims grew larger, the Makkans started persecuting them, thinking that it would stop the further spread of Islam. The Holy Prophet, peace and blessings of Allah be upon him, was no exception. His house was stoned. On many occasions, rubbish was thrown on him, as he passed by. In spite of all this opposition, the message of Islam continued to spread.

Seeing this the non-believers were greatly worried. They sent a deputation to the Prophet's uncle and guardian, Abu Taalib.

They said to him, 'You are one of our chiefs, and for your sake we have so far spared your nephew. We demand that he should refrain from saying anything against our idols. If he agrees to this, there is no dispute between us and him. If you cannot persuade him to do this, then one of two things must happen. Either you will have to give up your nephew, or all your people will give you up'.

Abu Taalib was much upset. He sent for the Holy Prophet, peace and blessings of Allah be upon him, and told him what had happened. The Prophet listened to him carefully. Tears came to his eyes. He did not want his uncle to suffer because of him. He said, 'I ask you not to give up your people. I ask you not to stand by me. God is my witness, that even if they were to place the sun in my right hand and the moon in my left, I would not desist from preaching the truth with which God has sent me'.

Hearing this bold reply from his nephew, Abu Taalib said, 'Son of my brother, go your way. Do your duty as you see it. Let my people give me up. I will stand by you'.

Study Questions

QUESTION 1: What was the name of the Prophet's uncle?

YOUR RESPONSE: _____

QUESTION 2: Why did the people of Makkah visit him?

YOUR RESPONSE: _____

_____

QUESTION 3: What was their demand?

YOUR RESPONSE: _____

_____

QUESTION 4: What was the Prophet's reply to his uncle?

YOUR RESPONSE: _____

_____

THE JOURNEY TO TA'IF

There was so much opposition to the Holy Prophet in Makkah that it seemed impossible for him to preach to the Makkans. Whenever he was out in the street, abuses were hurled at him and he was ridiculed. Sometimes rubbish was thrown at him. The Prophet did not mind this sort of ill-treatment as long as he had the chance to preach, but there came a time when he could preach no longer in Makkah. He decided to go to some other town to convey the Divine message.

He went to Ta'if, some sixty miles away. Zaid accompanied him on this journey. The Holy Prophet met the chiefs of the town and invited them to Islam, but they ignored his message. Neither the chiefs nor their people would listen to him. He tried to address some people at one place, but found hatred in

their hearts for him, so much so, that they set vagabonds and layabouts on him, who pelted him with stones and drove him out of the town. Zaid was hit by stones and was injured. The Holy Prophet was also hit and began to bleed from the injuries to his legs. They hurried away from the town, but still people came after them. The chase went on until both were several miles out of Ta'if.

The Holy Prophet was very sad and disappointed at the treatment he had received from the people of Ta'if. They sat down at one place to rest. Suddenly an angel appeared and asked him, 'Would you like that all those who treated you badly be destroyed?'

The Holy Prophet replied, 'No, I hope that their children at least would accept Islam and worship the One, True God'.

The place where he was resting, was a vineyard belonging to two Makkans. When the owners of the vineyard noticed his injuries, they took pity on him and sent a Christian slave Addas by name, with a tray of ripe grapes to him. Addas was so moved by the sight of the Holy Prophet and was so impressed with his talk, that he became a Muslim. He began to kiss his head, hands and feet and asked for his blessings. The Prophet stayed for a while and then started his journey back to Makkah.

Study Questions

QUESTION 1: Why did the Prophet go to Ta'if?

YOUR RESPONSE:

QUESTION 2: How far is Ta'if from Makkah?

YOUR RESPONSE:

QUESTION 3: Who accompanied the Holy Prophet on this journey?

YOUR RESPONSE:

QUESTION 4: What treatment did he receive from the people of Ta'if?

YOUR RESPONSE: _____

_____

_____

_____

_____

_____

QUESTION 5: What did the angel say to the Holy Prophet?

YOUR RESPONSE: _____

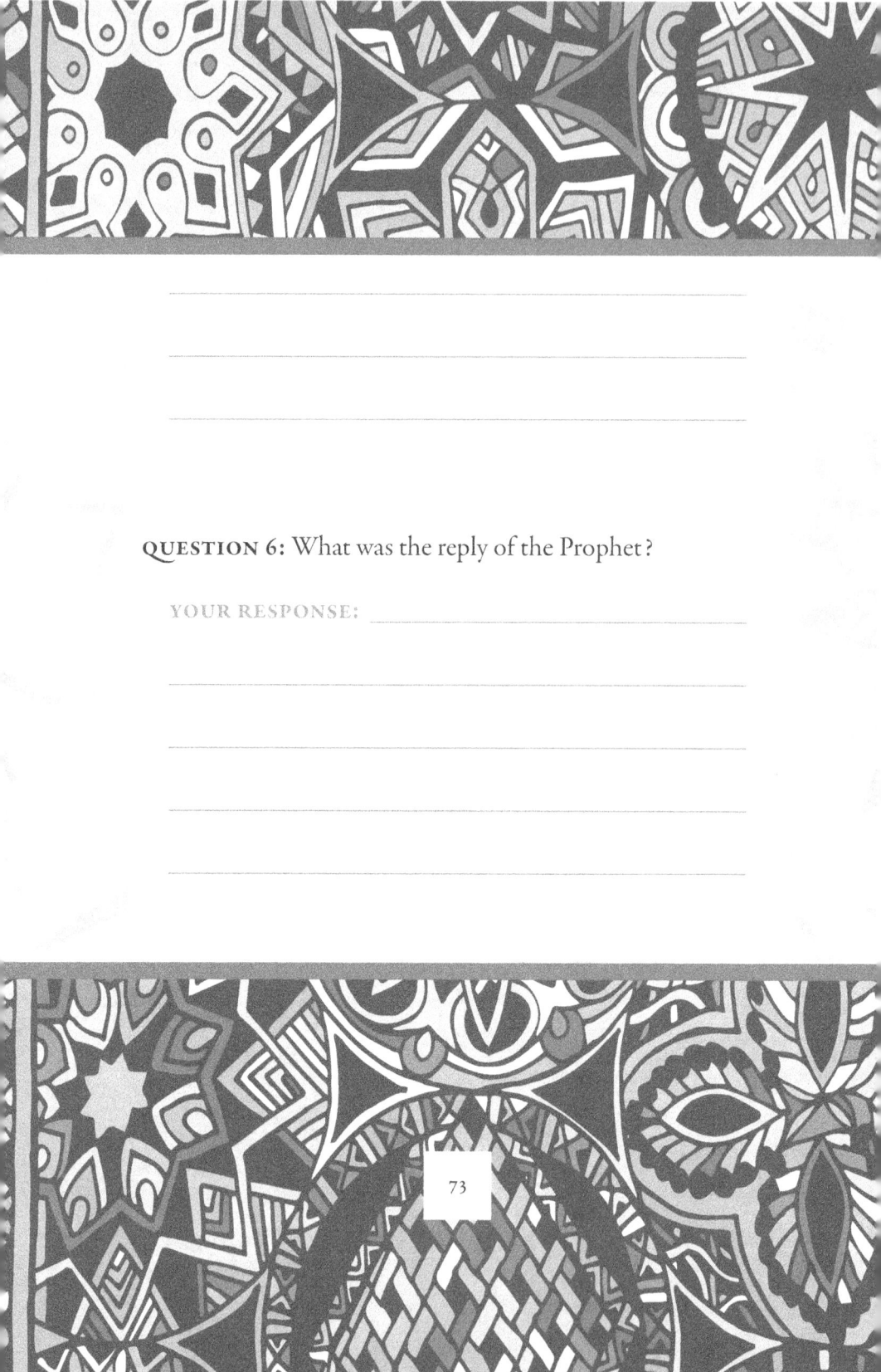

QUESTION 6: What was the reply of the Prophet?

YOUR RESPONSE:

FEAR NOT, GOD IS WITH US

When the opponents of the Holy Prophet[saw] saw that Islam was making progress and that there was a steady increase in the number of Muslims, they were greatly provoked. They had employed all means of persecution to stop progress, as they considered Islam to be a definite threat to their way of life and to their beliefs and doctrines. No one was secure against persecution, not even the Prophet[saw] himself. The worst affected were the slaves who accepted Islam. Their masters inflicted unbearable torments upon them in vain attempt to force them to renounce Islam. They Were taken out during the scorching heat of the mid-day sun and were made to lie down on their bare backs on the burning sands and rocks, while stones were heaped on them. Boys were incited to make them victims of their cruel sport. They would tie ropes to the ankles or the neck of a slave and drag him through the streets paved with rough stones, leaving him with bruises and cuts.

As the Muslims had a strong faith, they bore all those sufferings with patience and remained steadfast. There came a time when life was made so impossible for them in Makkah, that they decided to migrate. They went to Yathrib, where Islam had spread already and Muslims were living peacefully.

Family after family left the city and made their way to Yathrib secretly. Sometimes a whole street would be emptied in the course of one night. In the morning the Makkans would see

the doors locked and would realise that the residents had fled. At last the Holy Prophet[saw] and a few of his companions were left at Makkah. They were also ready to leave, and were waiting for God's command.

The Makkans saw all this. They did not want the Muslims to prosper in Yathrib. So all the chiefs of Makkah gathered for consultation. They decided to kill the Prophet[saw] without further delay. In order to spread the responsibility among them, they decided to appoint one man from each tribe to do the job. They fixed a particular night for this purpose.

At this point the Prophet[saw] received God's command to leave Makkah, and it so happened that the night fixed for his departure was the one that his opponents had chosen for their evil design. Abu Bakr, having learned from the Prophet[saw] of the decision to leave Makkah, begged for permission to accompany him. The Prophet[saw] gave his assent.

The following evening the Prophet[saw] left his home as soon as it was dark. While those who intended to kill him were

gathering round the house, the Holy Prophet[saw] went away unnoticed. Abu Bakr also joined him and the two made their way out of the city. They went up one of the surrounding hills and took shelter in a cave called 'Thaur'. This cave had a very narrow entrance, so that a person would have to lie flat to crawl into it. It was not a safe place to hide as there was considerable danger from reptiles of all kinds.

In the morning when the people of Makkah learned that the Prophet[saw] had left, they sent a party in search of him. They announced that anyone who would bring him back dead or alive would receive a reward of one hundred camels. Following the footprints, they arrived at the mouth of the cave in which the Holy Prophet[saw] and Abu Bakr had taken shelter. The tracker announced that the marks of the footsteps of the fugitives did not go any further. Therefore, they had either sunk into the earth or had risen to the sky. The whole party ridiculed him at his remarks. They did not bother to look inside the cave, as they knew that the cave was not a safe place of refuge. Who on earth

would take the risk of serious bodily harm and possibly death, from the poisonous snakes and vipers inside the cave?

Abu Bakr got very worried when he saw them standing there, at the mouth of the cave. He could hear their voices. He could even see them moving about, through a narrow opening of the cave. He whispered to the Holy Prophet[saw] his fear that they might be discovered. The Holy Prophet[saw] replied calmly, 'Grieve not, for Allah is with us'.

Abu Bakr was reassured. The Makkans thought that they had missed the track and returned frustrated.

The Holy Prophet[saw] and Abu Bakr spent two nights and two days in the cave. Then they left and after a few days' journey reached Yathrib, where the Muslims gave them a warm welcome.

Study Questions

QUESTION 1: Why did Muslims leave Makkah?

YOUR RESPONSE: _____

_____

_____

_____

QUESTION 2: What plan did the Makkans adopt to get rid of the Holy Prophet^{saw}?

YOUR RESPONSE: _____

_____

_____

_____

QUESTION 3: How did he manage to escape from the enemy?

YOUR RESPONSE: _____

_____

_____

_____

QUESTION 4: Who accompanied him on the journey from Makkah to Yathrib?

YOUR RESPONSE: _____

_____

QUESTION 5: Where did they take shelter?

YOUR RESPONSE: _____

_____

_____

QUESTION 6: Why did the pursuing party not look into the cave?

YOUR RESPONSE: _____

_____

_____

_____

QUESTION 7: What reward was offered by the Makkans?

YOUR RESPONSE:

QUESTION 8: What did Abu Bakr say to the Holy Prophet^{saw} while in the cave?

YOUR RESPONSE:

QUESTION 9: What was the Prophet's[saw] reply?

YOUR RESPONSE: _____

_____

_____

_____

_____

_____

QUESTION 10: How long did the Holy Prophet[saw] and Abu Bakr remain in the cave?

YOUR RESPONSE: _____

_____

_____

_____

_____

THE PROPHECY ABOUT THE GOLD BANGLES

The Holy Prophet^{saw} was naturally very sad when he was forced to leave Makkah, the city where he had been born and brought up, the only home he had known. It was the place where his forefathers had lived and died, and where he had received the Divine Call. With these thoughts in mind, he had a last look at the city and said, 'Makkah, you are dearer to me than any other place on earth, but your people would not let me live here'.

For two days and two nights, the Holy Prophet^{saw} and Abu Bakr remained hidden in the cave. Then they proceeded in the direction of Yathrib. Suraaqah bin Maalik, who had heard of the reward announced by the *Quraish,* was on the look-out for them. One day he spotted two mounted camels heading north. He guessed that those were the persons he was looking for. So he spurred his horse in their direction. He did not go very far when the legs of his horse sank in the sand and he fell down. He got up, took out his arrows and consulted his luck in the old Arab fashion. The arrow showed bad luck. But the temptation of the reward was so great that he mounted his horse again and set out after the two. As he came closer, the legs of his horse sank again in the sand and he fell down. Again he consulted his arrows, and they gave the same message of bad luck. Suraaqah changed his mind. He realised that the party was under Divine

protection. So he called out to them and told them of his evil intention and of his change of heart. As he was returning, the Prophet[saw] said to him, 'Suraaqah, how will you feel with the gold bangles of the king of Iran on your wrists?'

Suraaqah was amazed to hear this prophecy. Later he accepted Islam and lived in Madinah.

It so happened that during the *Khilafat* of Umar, Iran and its treasures fell to Muslims, including the gold bangles which the king used to wear on state functions. Umar sent for Suraaqah and asked him to wear the gold bangles.

'How can I wear them?' said Suraaqah, 'The wearing of gold is forbidden in Islam for men'.

Umar said, 'I know, but you should wear them in order to fulfil the prophecy of the Holy Prophet'.

Suraaqah put on the gold bangles and thus the prophecy made by the Holy Prophet[saw], years earlier, was fulfilled to the letter.

Study Questions

QUESTION 1: Why did the Prophet[saw] feel sad when he was leaving Makkah?

YOUR RESPONSE: _____

_____

_____

QUESTION 2: What words did he utter on that occasion?

YOUR RESPONSE: _____

_____

QUESTION 3: Who was Suraaqah?

YOUR RESPONSE: _____

_____

_____

QUESTION 4: Why did Suraaqah change his mind?

YOUR RESPONSE: _____

_____

_____

QUESTION 5: How was the prophecy about the gold bangles fulfilled?

YOUR RESPONSE: _____

_____

_____

_____

TWO YOUNG EAGLES

When the Holy Prophet^{saw} was forced to leave Makkah, he decided to settle in Yathrib, later known as Madinatun-Nabi or Madinah. Islam had already spread to this city, and there was a fairly large Muslim community when he arrived there. More and more people joined the fold of Islam. Soon Madinah became the first Muslim city.

When the Makkans learned that the Prophet^{saw} had been warmly received by the people of Madinah, and that Islam was making progress among the tribes there, they resolved to attack Madinah. They raised an army of one thousand armed fighters, most of whom were well experienced in warfare, and started marching towards Madinah, one year after the Holy Prophet^{saw} reached there. When the news reached the Holy Prophet^{saw}, he took counsel with his people, and gathered 313 men to fight the enemy. Most of these men had no experience of fighting. Some of them were mere boys in their teens. The Muslims were ill-equipped. There were only two horses and a few camels among the whole lot.

As this was the first battle between Muslims and the non-believers, every Muslim fighter, young or old, was eager to show bravery in battle. All of them were determined to die in defence of their faith. Such was the motley crowd, led by the Holy Prophet^{saw}, which came out of the city to meet the enemy. The two forces met at a place called 'Badr'.

One of the few experienced fighters in the Muslim force was Abdur-Rahman bin Auf. He was happy because the day, he was longing for, had come. He could now show his skill and valour on the battlefield.

As the Holy Prophet[saw] arranged the Muslims for the battle, Abdur-Rahman looked towards his sides and was greatly disappointed to see two young boys on either side of him. He felt exposed on both sides and would have to take good care of himself. As he was contemplating the situation, one of the boys nudged him and said, 'Uncle, where is Abu Jahl, who used to persecute the Holy Prophet[saw] and harass the Muslims?'

Abdur-Rahman had not yet shown him Abu Jahl, when the boy on the other side whispered the same question in his ear. Abdur-Rahman raised his finger in order to point out Abu Jahl,

BATTLEFIELD OF BADR

who was on horseback, well armed and right in the heart of the Makkan army.

No sooner did Abdur-Rahman point out Abu Jahl than the two boys dashed forward into the ranks of the enemy, with the speed of an eagle. The attack was so sudden that everybody was shaken. The soldiers and the guards round Abu Jahl were taken by surprise. They attacked the boys in order to prevent them from going further towards their leader. One of the boys received a blow on his shoulder. His arm was cut and hung loose by his side, yet he continued to fight with one hand. The other boy was also injured, but they did not retreat. They went on and on until they reached Abu Jahl. They pounced upon him with such force that the experienced commander fell to the ground, and was fatally wounded.

The two young brave Muslim boys did what surprised even the best among the Muslim fighters.

Study Questions

1. **QUESTION 3:** When was the battle of Badr fought?

    YOUR RESPONSE: _____

    _____

    _____

QUESTION 2: What was the number of Makkans who marched towards Madinah?

YOUR RESPONSE:

QUESTION 3: How many Muslims went out to intercept the Makkans?

YOUR RESPONSE:

QUESTION 4: Who was Abu Jahl? How was he killed?

YOUR RESPONSE:

QUESTION 5: Describe the condition of the Makkan force as compared to Muslims.

YOUR RESPONSE:

THE UNDECIDED BATTLE

To wipe out the shame and disgrace suffered at the defeat of 'Badr', the Quraish announced that they would attack Madinah again. They made preparations on a large scale and after one year attacked with a much larger and stronger force. Their army consisted of three thousand fighters, seven hundred of whom were in armour, and two hundred mounted on horses.

When the news of the approach of this force reached the Holy Prophet, he called his followers and held a council. With one thousand men at his command, the Holy Prophet came out to defend the city. At a short distance from Madinah, they camped for the night. In the morning when the Holy Prophet was making his rounds, he discovered that a certain number

of Jews of Madinah had also joined in. As they were under no obligation to fight outside the city, the Prophet sent them back.

Abdullah bin Ubayy was also among the Muslims who came out to fight against the Makkans. He was a hypocrite. He objected to the Prophet's decision to send the Jews back. He felt that the Muslims were no match for the Makkans. As soon as the Jews left, he also withdrew with three hundred of his supporters. The Holy Prophet was thus left with 700 only under his command, out of which only one hundred were in armour.

The Muslim army reached a place called Uhud. The Holy Prophet posted fifty of his men on a narrow hilly pass at the back and told them that they must guard the pass and on no account should they leave their post without receiving his orders. With the remaining force, he faced an army nearly five times as large and many times better in equipment.

Soon after the battle began, the Makkans retreated and started running away from the battlefield, hotly pursued by the Muslims. Seeing this, the Muslims who were posted at the pass became eager to join in the pursuit. Their commander reminded them of the clear orders of the Prophet and tried in vain to stop them from going after the fleeing enemy. However most of them left saying that there was no point in staying there while the enemy was in flight.

One of the Makkan commanders, Khalid bin Waleed, who later became a great Muslim general, saw this poorly guarded pass. He drew the attention of his colleague, Amr bin Aas towards it. Both these generals stopped their fleeing warriors and headed towards the pass from behind the hills. They killed the remaining Muslim guards and attacked the Muslim forces from the rear. The attack was so sudden that for some time everything was in a state of confusion. The Muslims were scattered all over the field. Some of them had already withdrawn from the battlefield thinking that the enemy had run away. Only a handful of his Companions remained with the Holy Prophet to repel the attack. The fleeing Makkans stopped and returned when they heard the war cries of their fellows, who had attacked the Muslims from the rear.

The Holy Prophet was in great danger. Those around him were falling one by one under the intensive attack of the enemy. There also came a volley of arrows directed at the Prophet. Talha, a faithful friend of the Prophet stretched out his arm to shield the face of the Holy Prophet from the arrows. Arrow after arrow struck his arm and pierced through his hand. He saw blood, felt pain, but did not let his arm drop. Ultimately he lost the use of his arm. Stones were also hurled at the Prophet. One hit him in the face. Then came another blow which drove the rings of his helmet right into his cheek. He fell down unconscious among the heap of dead Muslim fighters. The Makkans thought that they had killed the Prophet and withdrew calling it a day. The Muslims also thought for a while that he had died, and the rumour spread like wild fire, so much so, that the women and children of Madinah ran out in the direction of 'Uhud' to discover the truth.

When the remaining Muslim fighters realised what had

happened, they gathered round the spot where the Holy Prophet had fallen. The Prophet soon returned to consciousness.

Abu Sufyaan, the enemy commander, who was then rejoicing with his men, shouted, 'We have killed Muhammad'. The Holy Prophet told his followers to keep quiet. As there was no reply from the Muslim side, Abu Sufyaan became certain of the death of the Prophet. He cried aloud again, 'We have killed Abu Bakr'. Still no reply came from the Muslims. Then the enemy commander raised his voice and said, 'We have killed Umar as well'. The Holy Prophet again told the Muslims to remain quiet. Abu Sufyaan then said, 'Hurray, we have killed all three and raised the national cry in praise of Hubal, their god, saying, 'Glory be to Hubal'. At this stage, the Holy Prophet told the Muslims to reply. 'What shall we say, O Messenger of Allah?' they asked. 'Say, Allah alone is Great and Mighty. He alone is High and Honoured', said the Holy Prophet.

Hearing this reply the enemy was disappointed to know that the Holy Prophet, Abu Bakr and Umar were all alive.

Though the Muslims were now very small in number, yet the Makkans dared not attack again and returned to Makkah.

Study Questions

QUESTION 1: Compare the condition of the Muslims with that of the Makkans at the battle of Uhud.

YOUR RESPONSE:

QUESTION 2: Why did the Muslims leave the pass unguarded?

YOUR RESPONSE: _____

_____

_____

_____

QUESTION 3: Who were the Makkan commanders who attacked the Muslim army from the rear?

YOUR RESPONSE: _____

_____

_____

QUESTION 4: Who was Talha? Describe his act of bravery in this battle.

YOUR RESPONSE: _____

_____

_____

QUESTION 5: What was Hubal? Why did Abu Sufyaan raise the cry, 'Glory be to Hubal'?

YOUR RESPONSE:

QUESTION 6: What was the Prophet's reply to that cry?

YOUR RESPONSE:

QUESTION 7: Who was Abdullah bin Ubayy? What role did he play in this battle?

YOUR RESPONSE: _____

_____

_____

QUESTION 8: What do you think, was the cause which turned clear Muslim victory into confusion in this battle?

YOUR RESPONSE: _____

_____

_____

A STRANGE CONTEST

When the Muslims came out of Madinah to fight against the Makkan army in the battle of Uhud, some youngsters also accompanied them in their zeal to fight for Islam. The Holy Prophet[saw] found them out during his inspection and asked them to go back. Among them were Zaid bin Thabit, Abu Saeed Khudri, Samurah bin Jundub and Raafi bin Khudaij.

Zaid was an orphan. He was in his teens when the battle of Uhud was fought. He offered himself for the battle, but was sent back by the Prophet[saw].

Abu Saeed Khudri was thirteen years old. He was also very keen to take part in the battle. His father approached the Holy Prophet[saw] and submitted to him, 'Messenger of Allah, my son

is very strong. I am sure he will fight well, if he is permitted to take part in the battle'.

The Holy Prophet[saw] looked at the boy again, praised his spirit, but decided that he should go back as he was too young to take part in the fighting.

Raafi was also of the same age. His father, too, went to the Holy Prophet[saw] and said, 'Messenger of Allah, my son Raafi is a very good archer. He will be of great help to us if you let him stay on'.

When the Holy Prophet[saw] turned towards Raafi, he stood on his toes to make himself look taller than he actually was. The Prophet[saw] smiled and allowed him to stay.

Samurah was also rejected because of his young age. He complained to his father saying, 'The Holy Prophet[saw] allowed Raafi to take part in the battle, but rejected me, while I am stronger than him. I can surely beat him in a wrestling bout'.

This was reported to the Holy Prophet[saw]. The Prophet[saw] called both boys and asked Samurah to prove his claim.

The wrestling bout began and in no time Samurah threw Raafi to the ground. The Holy Prophet[saw] smiled and permitted Samurah to join the force as well.

During the battle these youngsters fought very bravely. Raafi proved to be a good archer, but in the course of the battle, an arrow pierced his chest and injured him. An attempt was made to extract it, but failed. The point of the arrow broke inside his body. He recovered from the injury but the wound reopened in his old age and proved fatal.

Study Questions

QUESTION 1: Name some of the youngsters who went along with the Muslim army.

YOUR RESPONSE: _____

_____

_____

QUESTION 2: Why did the Holy Prophet[saw] reject them?

YOUR RESPONSE: _____

_____

_____

_____

QUESTION 3: Why was Raafi allowed to stay on?

YOUR RESPONSE: _____

_____

QUESTION 4: How did Samurah succeed in being included among the fighters?

YOUR RESPONSE: _____

_____

_____

QUESTION 5: What happened to Raafi during the fight?

YOUR RESPONSE: _____

_____

_____

_____

TWO MARTYRS

This is a story of two Companions of the Holy Prophet[saw]. Their names were Zaid and Khubaib. Both of them had dedicated their lives to the cause of Islam.

It so happened that the representatives of the two tribes 'Adul' and 'Qarah' of Banu Lahyaan approached the Holy Prophet[saw] and told him that their tribes were interested in Islam. They requested him to send to them some Muslim teachers, so that they could learn more about Islam. The Holy Prophet[saw] agreed to send ten of his Companions with them. Zaid and Khubaib were among them.

When this party reached the territory of Banu Lahyaan, they found that they had been betrayed. Actually, Banu Lahyaan were arch enemies of Islam. They devised this scheme

with the intention of killing the Muslim scholars. This small party was attacked by two hundred men with arrows and other weapons. The Muslims climbed up a near-by hill and challenged the enemy. The non-believers offered to spare their lives if they would come down and surrender themselves. The Muslims did not believe them and chose to fight to the finish. So when an attack was launched on them, they fought bravely. But being very few in number they could not do much. Seven of them fell down dead. To the remaining three they again said, 'Surrender and your lives will be spared'. This time they surrendered.

As soon as they came down, they were made prisoners, and were tied down with ropes. One of these three said that that was a breach of agreement and refused to go with them. At this they attacked him and killed him on the spot.

The remaining two captives, namely Zaid and Khubaib were taken by them to Makkah and were sold as slaves. The Makkan who bought Khubaib, wanted to murder him so as to avenge his own father's death, who had been killed in the battle of Badr.

One day when Khubaib was doing some work with a sharp knife, his master's child came close to him to see what he was doing. Khubaib took the child in his lap and began to talk to him. When the mother of the child noticed this, she was terrified in case the prisoner should harm the child. Khubaib saw the worried face of the mother. He said to her, 'Don't be afraid. I do not intend any harm to the child. We Muslims do not play false'

The woman was so impressed by what she heard, that she used to say afterwards, 'I have never seen a prisoner like Khubaib'.

Khubaib remained in captivity for many days. At last the day came when they decided to kill him. Hundreds of people gathered round him, when he was being led to his execution. They asked him his last wish. He requested them to allow him to say a short Prayer. They agreed to this. He said his Prayer quickly. When he finished, he said that he had wanted to prolong his supplication but did not do so, lest they should think he was afraid of death. Very confidently he began to recite:

'So long as I die a Muslim, I care not whether my headless body drops to the right or to the left. And why should I? My death is in the cause of God; if He wills, He can bless every part of my body'.

He had hardly finished, when the sword fell on his neck and his head fell.

Zaid, the other prisoner was also taken out to be executed. Just before he was killed, the chief of Makkah approached him and said, 'Would you not wish that Muhammad should be in your place today and you should be sitting secure among your family?'

Zaid, replied, 'God is my witness, I would rather die than that the Prophet[saw] should feel as much as the pricking sensation of a thorn in his foot in Madinah'.

Thus he also laid down his life for the cause of Islam.

Study Questions

QUESTION 1: Name the two tribes which made a request to the Holy Prophet^{saw} for teachers.

YOUR RESPONSE: _____

_____

QUESTION 2: How many teachers were sent to Banu Lahyaan?

YOUR RESPONSE: _____

_____

_____

QUESTION 3: What happened to the Muslim teachers when they reached the territory of Banu Lahyaan?

YOUR RESPONSE:

QUESTION 4: Why was the mother of the child so worried to see the child in Khubaib's lap?

YOUR RESPONSE:

QUESTION 5: Why did Khubaib say his Prayer quickly?

YOUR RESPONSE: _____

_____

_____

QUESTION 6: What did the chief of Makkah say to Zaid?

YOUR RESPONSE: _____

_____

_____

_____

QUESTION 7: What was Zaid's reply?

YOUR RESPONSE: _____

_____

_____

_____

SWORD OF ALLAH

When the news reached Madinah that some of the Christian tribes were gathering a large army on the Syrian border, the Holy Prophet[saw] sent fifteen men as a scouting party to arrange a truce with them. When this party reached there, they found that the enemy was in no mood to talk. They were attacked and killed.

The Holy Prophet[saw] was much grieved to learn this. He decided to send an armed force to avenge the unjustified massacre of the scouting party. As he was planning this, he learned that the enemy forces has dispersed. He therefore postponed the plan, and sent an envoy instead, with a letter to the chief of the Ghassaan tribe who ruled Busra. In this letter he complained about the border incidents. This letter was carried by a Companion of the Holy Prophet[saw], named Al-Haarith.

Al-Haarith was also arrested and killed by the local Ghassaan chief while he was on his way. This was another act of provocation. The Holy Prophet[saw], therefore, raised a force of three thousand fighters and sent them to take action against that Christian tribe. Zaid bin Haarithah was appointed as the Commander of this force.

The Holy Prophet[saw] gave instructions that if Zaid were killed, Ja'afar ibn Abi Taalib would take over, and should Ja'afar die, Abdullah bin Rawaahah would succeed him. Should Abdullah die, Muslims were to choose their own commander.

A Jew who heard these directions, said to Zaid, 'Take it from me, if Muhammad is true, you will not return alive'. Zaid replied, 'I may return or not, but surely Muhammad is the true Prophet of God'.

When this force arrived at the Syrian border, they learned that the Roman Emperor had brought a large army of one hundred thousand soldiers against the Muslims. Moreover, another hundred thousand warriors were raised by the local tribes to support the Emperor against the Muslims.

Despite the fact that the Muslims were grossly outnumbered, they, being inspired by faith and the righteousness of their cause, fought bravely.

Just as the Prophet[saw] had foretold, first Zaid was killed in the battlefield, then Ja'afar and Abdullah were also killed, each in turn, and the command of the Muslim force fell to the lot of Khalid bin Waleed.

When Ja'afar was in command and was holding the flag in his hand, his right arm was cut off. He, therefore, held the flag

with his left hand. Soon he lost his left arm. He held the flag between the stumps pressed to his chest.

Khalid was an experienced soldier. When he took command of the Muslim force, he rearranged them. Those who were in the rear were brought to the front, and those who were fighting on the right, were brought to the left. The enemy was baffled by such tactics. They thought that the Muslim force had been reinforced. Khalid then skilfully disengaged his men and brought them back without serious loss.

The whole progress of the battle was shown to the Holy Prophet[saw] in a vision. He collected the Muslims of Madinah and told them, 'Our soldiers are coming back victorious. They fought bravely. First Zaid, then Ja'afar, then Abdullah died as commanders. Pray for them all. After their death the flag was held by Khalid bin Waleed. He is a sword among the swords of Allah. So he delivered his force from a difficult situation and they are on their way back'. It is after this incident that Khalid became known as the 'Sword of Allah'.

Study Questions

QUESTION 1: What was the cause of this battle?

YOUR RESPONSE: _____

_____

_____

QUESTION 2: Who was the messenger sent to the chief of the Ghassaan tribe?

YOUR RESPONSE: _____

_____

QUESTION 3: Why were three men named as the commanders of the Muslim force?

YOUR RESPONSE: _____

_____

_____

QUESTION 4: Name the three commanders who were appointed by the Holy Prophet[saw].

YOUR RESPONSE:

QUESTION 5: Who was chosen as the commander when all three died?

YOUR RESPONSE:

QUESTION 6: What were the tactics used by Khalid bin Waleed in this battle?

YOUR RESPONSE:

QUESTION 7: Describe Ja'afar's steadfastness in the middle of the fighting.

YOUR RESPONSE: _____

_____

_____

_____

QUESTION 8: What was the title bestowed upon Khalid bin Waleed by the Holy Prophet[saw]?

YOUR RESPONSE: _____

_____

_____

THE SPIRIT OF SACRIFICE

At the time of the battle of Tabuk, the Holy Prophet[saw] called for contributions, so that he could make the necessary preparations for the battle. There was a striking response to his appeal. The examples of Abu Bakr and Umar were typical. Both were wealthy enough to contribute a substantial sum towards the fund.

Umar used to say that Abu Bakr always outdid him in sacrifice for the cause of Islam. On this occasion he was determined to surpass him. With this in mind, he came home, collected all his belongings and divided them into two equal halves. He left one half at home and took the other to the Holy Prophet[saw].

The Holy Prophet[saw] was much pleased and asked him, 'Umar! Did you leave anything at home for your family?' 'Yes,

Messenger of Allah, I have left at home half of what I possessed', replied Umar. The Holy Prophet[saw] thanked him and prayed for him.

In the meantime, Abu Bakr also arrived with his contribution. The Holy Prophet[saw] asked, 'Abu Bakr! What have you left at home?'

He answered 'Only the name of Allah and his Messenger.

The Holy Prophet[saw] thanked him and prayed for him. Umar realized that he would never be able to outdo Abu Bakr in such matters.

Study Questions

QUESTION 1: For what purpose did the Holy Prophet[saw] raise the fund?

YOUR RESPONSE:

QUESTION 2: What was Umar's wish on this occasion?

YOUR RESPONSE:

QUESTION 3: How much did Umar contribute?

YOUR RESPONSE:

QUESTION 4: How much did Abu Bakr contribute?

YOUR RESPONSE:

اَللّٰهُ

WHO CAN SAVE YOU NOW?

On one occasion, in the course of a journey, the Holy Prophet[saw] and his Companions decided to take rest among a grove of trees, to avoid the heat of the sun. The party spread themselves out and lay down to rest in the shade. The Holy Prophet[saw] also hung up his sword by the branch of a tree and lay down to rest.

It so happened that a bitter enemy of the Prophet[saw] had been following the party for some distance. He considered this a good opportunity to kill him. He, therefore, sneaked up to the Holy Prophet[saw] and finding him unguarded, took his sword from the tree, and drew it to attack him. The Holy Prophet[saw] woke up in surprise. The man lifted the sword up and said, 'Who can save you from me?'

'Allah' said the Prophet[saw] very calmly.

The sword fell from the enemy's hand, when he heard this. The Holy Prophet[saw] picked it up, moved away from under him, and took hold of the enemy. The position was now reversed.

'Who can save you now?', said the Holy Prophet[saw].

'No one', exclaimed the man in terror.

'Why do you not say 'Allah' ', asked the Holy Prophet[saw].

Hearing the noise of the scuffle, some of the Companions of the Holy Prophet[saw] rushed to the spot and found the two in this situation. The Holy Prophet[saw] explained to them what had happened.

Then the Prophet[saw] asked the man, 'What do you think should be done to you?

He replied, 'Be a generous captor'.

The Holy Prophet[saw] said, 'Very well, you can go free'.

When the man returned to his tribe, he told them the whole incident and said that Muhammad (peace and blessings of Allah be upon him) was a man whose mercy and forgiveness were beyond belief. This led him and his tribe to accept Islam.

Study Questions

QUESTION 1: Why was the man following the Holy Prophet[saw] and his party?

YOUR RESPONSE:

QUESTION 2: What did he do when he found the Prophet[saw] asleep unguarded?

YOUR RESPONSE:

QUESTION 3: Why did the sword fall down from his hand?

YOUR RESPONSE: _____

_____

_____

QUESTION 4: What was the effect of the Prophet's[saw] generous treatment of his enemy?

YOUR RESPONSE: _____

_____

_____

_____

FEEDING THE GUEST IN DARKNESS

A guest is always welcome and honoured in a Muslim family. Arabs are famous for their hospitality. Even before the advent of the Holy Prophet[saw], hospitality was their national virtue. They would show great consideration and would slaughter the best animal for their guest.

Once a stranger came to Madinah. He went straight to the mosque where the Holy Prophet[saw] was sitting and told him that he was hungry. The Holy Prophet[saw] sent somebody to inquire whether there was any food in his house for the guest who had arrived. The reply came that there was nothing but water in the house. The Holy Prophet[saw] then inquired from his

Companions, whether anyone could take the guest home and feed and lodge him. One of the Companions offered to do so.

When they reached home, the Companion asked his wife if there was enough food in the house for the guest. His wife replied that there was only a little food in the house which was hardly enough for the children.

The Companion said that he had brought with him a guest who had been entrusted to him by the Holy Prophet[saw]. He asked her to lull the children to sleep and prepare the food for the guest. He told her that when the food was ready he would invite the guest inside, to share it with them. As soon as they sit down, he would manage to put out the light. He suggested that thereafter they should pretend to eat and make sounds as if they were swallowing the food.

They acted upon this plan. So the whole family remained hungry while the guest ate to his fill.

Next morning both of them went to the mosque. The Holy Prophet[saw] addressed the host and said, 'God in heaven smiled over the device which you adopted last night'.

Study Questions

QUESTION 1: Why did the Companion take the stranger to his house?

YOUR RESPONSE:

QUESTION 2: How did they manage to feed the guest?

YOUR RESPONSE:

QUESTION 3: What lesson do you draw from this story?

YOUR RESPONSE:

EQUAL JUSTICE

Once a woman of a very respectable *Quraish* family committed a theft and was sentenced to undergo the prescribed punishment. Some of the Companions of the Holy Prophet[saw] were much concerned that the carrying out of the sentence would disgrace the family of the culprit. They were therefore anxious that someone should intercede with the Holy Prophet[saw] on behalf of the woman and procure her pardon. They decided to ask Usaamah bin Zaid, who was greatly loved by the Holy Prophet[saw] to intercede on behalf of the woman.

Usaamah went to the Holy Prophet[saw] and made his submission as he had been requested. The Holy Prophet[saw] was much upset. He admonished Usaamah, 'Have you come to intercede in the matter of the infliction of a prescribed penalty?

People before you were ruined because of such discrimination. They would enforce the full rigour of the law against the poor and would let the well to do, go free. By Allah, in whose hands is my life, were my daughter Faatimah to commit an offence, I would strictly enforce the penalty prescribed by the law against her'.

Study Questions

QUESTION 1: What was the charge against the woman?

YOUR RESPONSE:

QUESTION 2: Why did the Companions decide to approach the Holy Prophet[saw]?

YOUR RESPONSE:

QUESTION 3: Who was sent to the Holy Prophet^{saw} to intercede on behalf of the woman?

YOUR RESPONSE:

QUESTION 4: What was the Prophet's^{saw} reply when Usaamah told him the wish of the *Quraish*?

YOUR RESPONSE:

NON-DISCRIMINATION

During the battle of Badr, many Makkans were taken prisoners. They were all tied up with ropes, so as to prevent their escape. Among the prisoners was Abbaas, an uncle of the Holy Prophet[saw], who was still a non-believer and had fought against the Muslims. He was also tied with ropes and was not far from the place where the Holy Prophet[saw] was resting for the night. The ropes were so tight that all the prisoners were groaning with pain. The Holy Prophet[saw] heard the groans of Abbaas, and was unable to sleep.

The Companions realised this and loosened the bonds of Abbaas. No more groans were coming from him now.

The Holy Prophet[saw] sent for someone and inquired how was it that he did not hear the groans of Abbaas any more. He

was told that the bonds of Abbaas were loosened, lest his groans should disturb the Holy Prophet[saw]. Thereupon, the Holy Prophet[saw] said, 'All prisoners should be treated alike. Loosen the bonds of all, or tighten the bonds of Abbaas as before'.

On this the Companions loosened the ropes of all the prisoners.

QUESTIONS

QUESTION 1: Who was Abbaas?

YOUR RESPONSE: _____

_____

_____

QUESTION 2: Why was he made a prisoner?

YOUR RESPONSE: _____

_____

_____

QUESTION 3: Why were his bonds loosened?

YOUR RESPONSE: _____

_____

_____

QUESTION 4: What was the Prophet's[saw] reaction to it?

YOUR RESPONSE: _____

_____

_____

_____

THE POISONED MEAT

Once a Jewish woman inquired from the Companions of the Holy Prophet^{saw}, 'What meat does the Holy Prophet fancy?' She was told that he preferred a shoulder of lamb or goat. She slaughtered a goat, cut it into small pieces and roasted them. Then she rubbed some deadly poison into them and took this meat to the Holy Prophet^{saw}.

The Holy Prophet^{saw} was coming back from the mosque after the evening Prayer, when he saw a woman standing in the dark with something in her hand. He approached her and asked, 'Is there anything I can do for you?' The woman replied, 'I have brought some roasted meat for you. I am sure you will be kind enough to accept it'.

THE HOLY PROPHET'S MOSQUE

The Holy Prophet^{saw} thanked the woman and asked one of his Companions to take the meat from her.

Later that evening, when he and his Companions sat down to have their meals together, the roasted meat, which the woman had presented to the Holy Prophet^{saw}, was also laid before them. As soon as the Prophet^{saw} tasted the meat, he suspected that it was poisoned. He stopped others from taking it, but a Companion named Bishr, had already swallowed some. Soon after this, Bishr became ill and died of the poison.

The Holy Prophet^{saw} sent for the woman and asked her if she had poisoned the meat.

'How can you say that?' said the woman.

The Holy Prophet^{saw} held a piece in his hand and said, 'My hands told me this', i.e., he knew as soon as he tasted it.

The woman confessed her guilt and begged for mercy.

'Why have you done this?', asked the Prophet^{saw}.

She replied, 'My people were at war with you and my relations were killed in the battle. I decided to poison you, believing that if you were an imposter, you would die and we should be safe, but if you were a true Prophet, God would save you.'

Hearing this reply the Prophet^{saw} forgave her, although she had earned the penalty of death.

Study Questions

QUESTION 1: What did the woman bring for the Holy Prophet[saw]?

YOUR RESPONSE: _____

_____

QUESTION 2: Why did she poison the meat?

YOUR RESPONSE: _____

_____

_____

QUESTION 3: Who died of poison?

YOUR RESPONSE: _____

_____

_____

QUESTION 4: Why did the Holy Prophet^{saw} forgive her?

YOUR RESPONSE: _____

_____

_____

_____

FEEDING A LARGE COMPANY

Abu Hurairah was a Companion of the Holy Prophet[saw], who, like several others, spent most of his time inside the mosque. They were known as *As'haab-us-Suffah* [the People of the Lounge]. They subsisted mostly on the charity of those who could spare some necessities of life for them. Their principal aim was to spend their time in the company of the Holy Prophet[saw], to listen to him, to observe his dealings with people and to convey this knowledge to others. As they hardly earned anything for their livelihood, they had often to go hungry for long periods.

Abu Hurairah's real name was Umair, but as he kept a cat and loved it very much, he became known by the name 'Abu Hurairah', meaning 'Father of cats'.

On one occasion he had nothing to eat for three days. The Holy Prophet[saw] happened to observe him and noticing his condition, inquired whether he was hungry.

Abu Hurairah replied, 'Yes, O Messenger of Allah'.

At that time there was no food in the Prophet's[saw] house, but a cup of milk was just brought for the Holy Prophet[saw] by somebody. The Prophet[saw] asked Abu Hurairah to go and call his brethren of the lounge.

Abu Hurairah was apprehensive that if all the other hungry ones were invited to share the milk with him, little of it would

be left for him, but there was no choice except to carry out the direction of the Holy Prophet[saw].

He, therefore, went to the mosque and called the others. Including himself there were seven of them. The Holy Prophet[saw] asked Abu Hurairah to present the cup of milk to each of them in turn, which he did. The Prophet[saw] urged each to drink to his fill. When all had drunk, the cup still had plenty of milk.

The Holy Prophet[saw] then said, 'Abu Hurairah! We are the only ones left now. Go ahead and drink to your fill'.

Abu Hurairah took the cup and began to drink the milk. The Holy Prophet[saw] went on urging him to drink more and more till he said that he could take no more.

He then handed the cup to the Holy Prophet[saw], who drank the milk that was left in it, and thanked God for His grace and mercy.

Study Questions

QUESTION 1: Who was Abu Hurairah? Why was he called by this name?

YOUR RESPONSE:

QUESTION 2: What was his real name?

YOUR RESPONSE:

QUESTION 3: How many people came to drink the milk?

YOUR RESPONSE: _____

_____

_____

QUESTION 4: Why was Abu Hurairah afraid that no milk might be left for him to drink?

YOUR RESPONSE: _____

_____

_____

QUESTION 5: Who were *As'haab-us-Suffah*?

YOUR RESPONSE: _____

_____

_____

_____

A LOVING RECOMPENSE

Towards the last days of the Holy Prophet[saw] in this world, he believed that his mission having been completed, he would be summoned back to God. He had therefore, been preparing his Companions by conveying to them in various ways, that his end was near.

One day he said to them, 'If a man makes a mistake, it is better that he should put it right in this life so that he should not be called to account for it, in the next. I say to you, therefore, that if I have done any wrong to any of you, he should come forward so that I may compensate him, as I do not wish to be reminded of my responsibility in the life hereafter'.

Those present were greatly moved to hear this. Their eyes were lowered in respect for him and some of them even wept. They remembered all his various gracious kindnesses to them. They knew that he never hurt anybody in his life. There was complete silence. Suddenly a voice came from one side. A man said, 'Messenger of Allah; Once when you were lining us up for battle, your elbow brushed against my back'.

The Holy Prophet[saw] turned his back towards the man and said, 'Come and take your revenge'.

The man advanced towards the Holy Prophet[saw] and said, 'Messenger of Allah, there is a difference. My back was bare when your elbow brushed against it but yours is covered'.

The Holy Prophet[saw] told him to raise the shirt from his back.

The man lifted up the shirt from the Prophet's[saw] back, and instead of hitting him, bent forward and kissed him on his back.

'What is this?' asked the Holy Prophet[saw].

The man replied, 'Your elbow did brush against me. But who could think of taking revenge from a kind person like you. You had now offered me a good opportunity of showing my love and devotion to you'.

The Companions who had hitherto been very angry with the man, now began to envy him.

Study Questions

QUESTION 1: What was the Holy Prophet's^{saw} invitation to the people?

YOUR RESPONSE:

QUESTION 2: Why were the Companions moved to hear him?

YOUR RESPONSE: _____

_____

_____

_____

QUESTION 3: Why did a Companion come forward to take revenge?

YOUR RESPONSE: _____

_____

_____

QUESTION 4: Why did the man kiss the back of the Holy Prophet?

YOUR RESPONSE: _____

_____

_____

KINDNESS TOWARDS PARENTS

One of the principal teachings of the Holy Qur'an is that one should show great respect to one's parents. In Islam, the love of parents and the duty owed to them stands higher than the love of children and the duty owed to them.

The Holy Qur'an says, 'Your Lord commanded that you worship none but Him, and that you show kindness to parents. If one or both of them attain old age in your life-time, never be harsh to them, nor reproach them, but always speak gently to them.

Be humbly tender with them and pray, My Lord, have mercy on them, even as they nourished me when I was a child'. (Holy Quran 17:24–25)

This shows that in old age, parents need to be tended as carefully and affectionately, as little children are looked after in their childhood, by their parents.

The Holy Prophet[saw] has said, 'Paradise lies at the feet of your mother'.

Once a man came to him and asked, 'Messenger of Allah! Which of my relations has the prior claim to my devotions?'

The Holy Prophet[saw] replied, 'Your mother'.

The man asked, 'And after her?'

The Holy Prophet[saw] replied, 'Your mother'.

The man asked a third time, 'And after my mother'.

He still replied, 'Your mother'.

When he asked for the fourth time, the Holy Prophet[saw] replied, 'Your father and after him other relations according to their degrees of kinship'.

When Makkah fell to the Muslims, and the Holy Prophet[saw] entered the city, Abu Bakr brought his father, a very old man, to meet him.

The Holy Prophet[saw] said to Abu Bakr, 'Why did you put your father to trouble by making him come to me? I would have gladly gone to see him myself'.

He has also said, 'Most unfortunate is the person who is granted an opportunity to serve his parents yet he fails to win Paradise through kindness towards them'.

الجنة تحت أقدام الأمهات

PARADISE LIES UNDER THE FEET OF MOTHERS

Study Questions

QUESTION 1: What did the Holy Prophet^{saw} say to Abu Bakr when he brought his father to see him?

YOUR RESPONSE: _____

_____

_____

QUESTION 2: What is meant by this saying of the Holy Prophet^{saw}, 'Paradise lies at the feet of your mother?'

YOUR RESPONSE: _____

_____

_____

LETTERS TO KINGS

After settling in Madinah the Holy Prophet[saw] sent letters to different rulers, inviting them to Islam. One such letter was sent to the Emperor of Abyssinia, who was a Christian. It ran as follows:

'In the name of Allah, the Gracious the Merciful.

From Muhammad, the Messenger of Allah to the Negus of Abyssinia.

May peace of God be upon you, O Emperor. I praise before you, the One and Only God. He and none other is worthy of worship. He is the King of kings, the Source of all excellence, free from all shortcomings. He is the Protector of all His creation and provides peace to His servants.

I bear witness that Jesus, son of Mary, was a Messenger of God, who was given to her, because of her devotion to Him, and in fulfilment of the promise made by God to her.

I invite you to join me in worshipping the One and Only God. I invite you also to follow me and believe in the God who sent me. I invite you and your armies to join the forces of the Almighty God. I hereby discharge my duty, as I have delivered to you the message of God. I have done so with a sincere heart and hope

you will value the sincerity which prompted this message. Whoever obeys the guidance of God, receives the blessings of God'.

When this letter reached the Emperor, he showed great respect for it. He took it into his hands, held it to his eyes and placed it reverently in an ivory box saying, 'As long as this letter is safe, my kingdom is safe'.

What the Emperor said, proved true, and though the Muslim Empire extended as far as India and China in one direction and Spain and Morocco in the other, the Negus continued to rule Abyssinia without any interference.

The Holy Prophet[saw] wrote a similar letter to the Emperor of Iran. When this letter reached him, he ordered an interpreter to read it to him. When the contents of the letter were explained to him, he rose in anger, took the letter in his hands and tore it to pieces. When this was reported to the Holy Prophet[saw], he said:

What the Emperor has done to my letter, God would do the same to his Empire.

But the King's fury was not over. He ordered the Viceroy of the Yemen to send soldiers to arrest the Holy Prophet[saw] and bring him to the court of the Emperor.

Accordingly the Viceroy sent two officers to Madinah to arrest the Prophet[saw]. He also gave them a letter addressed to the Prophet[saw] saying that he should accompany the messengers without delay.

On reaching Madinah, the officers told the Holy Prophet[saw] the purpose of their visit. They told him that if he refused to accompany them, he and his people would be destroyed. The Holy Prophet[saw] of Islam listened to them and told them to see him again the following morning. During the night he prayed to God Almighty, and there came the revelation, 'The son has murdered the father, this very night'.

In the morning, when those two soldiers came, the Holy

Prophet^{saw} told them what had been revealed to him. He also gave them a letter in reply, addressed to the Viceroy of the Yemen, mentioning the death of the Emperor at the hands of his son.

When the Viceroy received this reply he said, 'If this man is a true Prophet, it will be, as he says. If he is not, God help him and his country'.

Soon after, despatches from Iran confirmed the news that the Prophet^{saw} had conveyed to the Viceroy. It also contained directions revoking the order of the previous Emperor for the arrest of the Prophet^{saw}.

The Viceroy was so impressed that he and many of his friends accepted Islam.

Study Questions

QUESTION 1: What do you understand by the 'Negus'?

YOUR RESPONSE: _____

_____

_____

_____

_____

QUESTION 2: How did the Emperor of Abyssinia treat the letter of the Holy Prophet[saw]?

YOUR RESPONSE:

QUESTION 3: What was the reaction of the Emperor of Iran when the letter was read out to him?

YOUR RESPONSE:

QUESTION 4: What reply did the Prophet[saw] give to the two envoys of the Viceroy of Yemen?

YOUR RESPONSE:

QUESTION 5: What prophecy did the Prophet^saw of Islam make about the Emperor of Iran?

YOUR RESPONSE: _____

_____

_____

QUESTION 6: How did the Viceroy of Yemen accept Islam?

YOUR RESPONSE: _____

_____

_____

_____

POWER OF PRAYER

Prayer is the principal means by which man attains nearness to God Almighty. God says in the Holy Qur'an, 'When my servants ask you about Me, O Prophet, tell them I am close. I respond to the call of one who calls on Me. So they should respond to Me and believe in Me, that they may follow the right path'. (Holy Quran 2:187)

However powerful a man may be, his every action is dependant on the will and help of God, for which he has to turn to Him. Even the Holy Prophet[saw], like the rest, stood in need of His mercy and favour. He asked for His guidance and help in all matters and situations. Here are some instances which show how readily God heard his prayers.

I

At one time, due to lack of rain, Madinah was faced with famine. As the Holy Prophet^{saw} was delivering the Friday sermon, someone from among the audience called out, 'O Messenger of Allah! Cattle are dying for want of food and water. People are starving to death. Pray to God that He, through His mercy, sends us rain'.

The Holy Prophet^{saw} raised his hands and prayed to God for rain. The sky which had been absolutely clear, was suddenly covered with a sand storm. Thereafter dark clouds appeared, which brought heavy rain. As people reached their homes, their clothes were soaked. The rain continued to fall for a whole week. People became worried. They approached him again and said, 'Messenger of Allah!

The rain is creating havoc, houses are being destroyed. Pray to God that it may stop'.

The Holy Prophet^{saw} smiled and prayed again. Soon the clouds broke and Madinah was bright again.

II

Abu Hurairah's mother was a non-believer. He tried hard to convince her but she would not accept Islam. One day when he was talking to her, she spoke ill of the Prophet^{saw}. Abu Hurairah felt it very gravely. He went to the Holy Prophet^{saw} and after relating the whole incident, begged him to pray that God may grant her guidance. The Holy Prophet[saw] prayed to God.

Later on when Abu Hurairah returned home, he found the door of his house shut. He knocked at the door. His mother asked him to wait for a while. She finished her bath, changed her clothes, and with the words, 'There is none worthy of worship except Allah, and Muhammad is His Messenger', on her lips, opened the door.

Abu Hurairah was so pleased that he ran back to the Holy Prophet[saw] to tell him the good news.

III

Once Sa'ad bin Abi Waqqaas who accompanied the Holy Prophet[saw] to Makkah, fell seriously ill. There was no hope of his survival and his relatives got ready to write down his will. The Holy Prophet[saw] came to see him. Sa'ad said to him, 'Messenger of Allah! I am going to die in a town from where we had emigrated'.

The Holy Prophet[saw] consoled him and said, 'No, you will not die, if God wills'. Then he prayed three times for his recovery. His prayers were heard and Sa'ad soon recovered from his illness and lived for another fifteen years.

Study Questions

QUESTION 1: Give examples of the acceptance of the Prophet's^{saw} prayer.

YOUR RESPONSE: _____

_____

_____

QUESTION 2: Write a brief note on the importance of prayer.

YOUR RESPONSE: _____

_____

UMAR IN DISGUISE

I

When Abu Bakr died, Umar was elected as the second *Khalifah*. He was a tall, well-built man with fair complexion. He was a good speaker, a just ruler and very strict in discipline. He was a man of simple habits. Though, being a ruler, he handled vast treasures of gold, silver, jewels and valuables, yet his own cloak had many patches on it. He was the first ruler to organise administrative machinery in the country. He would visit the families of those who were serving in the cause of Allah and were away from home, to buy daily needs for them, write letters for them and even deliver their letters personally. He was

very anxious to know about the condition of his people. So he would go about unattended in the dark to find out for himself.

On one occasion, when he was walking in the dark, he heard some children crying. Attracted by the sound, he went to the tent from which it came. He saw a woman sitting before a fire. It appeared that the woman was cooking something, while her small children sat crying nearby. It was late for the children to have their meal.

Umar stepped up to the woman and inquired, 'What is in the pot on the fire?'

She explained that she had no food to give to the children and had placed the pot full of water and stones, on the fire in order to give them the impression that the food would be ready.

Umar was distressed to hear this. He hurried back to the State Store, picked up a bag of flour, meat, cooking oil and some dates and rushed back to the tent. His servant begged him to let him carry the load, but he refused saying, 'It is my responsibility. You would not carry my burden on the Day of Judgement'.

Arriving at the tent, he delivered the provisions to the woman and told her to prepare a meal. In the meantime the children had gone to sleep exhausted. Umar waited till the meal was ready and the children were awakened and fed. The woman thanked him for his kindness and by way of expressing gratitude said, 'It would be far better if you were the *Khalifah* of the Muslims, rather than that wretched Umar who is not aware of the condition of his people'.

Umar said, 'Well mother, Umar may not be so bad after all', and departed.

II

Once when Umar was making a round, he saw a Bedouin sitting outside the door of his tent. The *Khalifah* sat down and began to talk to him. Suddenly he heard a groan from inside the tent. Umar asked what the matter was.

The man told him that his wife was in labour.

Umar asked if there was any woman inside to attend to her. He replied that there was none.

The *Khalifah* hastened back home and took his wife with him to attend to the woman.

Presently the child was born and Umm-i-Kalsum, the wife of the *Khalifah* called out, *Ameerul-Momineen* (Leader of the faithful), congratulate your friend on the birth of a son'. When the man heard the words *Ameerul-Momineen,* he jumped up and stood respectfully before Umar.

'Never mind', said Umar, 'Come to see me tomorrow and I will sanction an allowance for the baby'.

Study Questions

QUESTION 1: Why did Umar make rounds in the dark?

YOUR RESPONSE: _____

_____

_____

_____

QUESTION 2: Why had the children not been fed?

YOUR RESPONSE: _____

_____

QUESTION 3: Why didn't Umar let the servant carry the provisions?

YOUR RESPONSE:

QUESTION 4: What did the *Khalifah* do to help the woman who was in labour?

YOUR RESPONSE: _____

_____

_____

_____

_____

QUESTION 5: How did the Bedouin come to know that the person who helped him was Umar, the *Khalifah*?

YOUR RESPONSE: _____

_____

_____

_____

_____

PREFERRING OTHERS TO ONESELF

The battle of Yarmuk was one of the greatest battles in the history of Islam. The Muslims were pitted against the might of the Byzantine Empire. Against an army of two hundred thousand soldiers, Khalid bin Waleed, the Muslim Commander had only a force of forty thousand under him. The Romans were much better equipped in every respect than the Muslims.

The battle lasted for six days, and on each day the fighting was more fierce than the previous day. Women also took an active part in the battle. Not only did they encourage the Muslim men to fight bravely against heavy odds, and admonish and rebuke them when they tried to run back from the battlefield, but also they actually assaulted them with tent poles and stones, thus forcing them back to face the enemy. Some of the Muslim women flung forward with their swords, and rushed into the thick of the battle, until they were ahead of the men. Umme Hakim, the daughter of Haarith; Asmaa, the daughter of Abu Bakr and Juwariyah, the sister of Muawiyah, were among the women who fought bravely in this battle.

It is recorded that the Muslims suffered a loss of four thousand men in this battle. Most of those who survived were injured, the wounds varying from light to severe. On the fourth day of the battle alone, about seven hundred Muslim soldiers

lost their eyes because of the arrows from the Roman army. As a result of this, the fourth day of the battle came to be known as the 'Day of the lost eyes'.

The Roman losses were much higher than those of the Muslims. It was estimated that about seventy thousand Roman soldiers died in the course of battle.

It is related that during this battle, a Muslim soldier Abu Jahm, went in search of his cousin, who was missing. He took water with him for the wounded soldiers. The injured and the dead lay scattered everywhere in the field. Abu Jahm found his cousin lying on the ground severely injured. He went near him and gave him some water to drink. As soon as the injured soldier brought the cup to his lips, he heard a cry for water from another wounded soldier, who lay nearby. He refused to drink the water and pointing towards the other soldier, told Abu Jahm, to take the water to him first.

Abu Jahm carried the water to the second soldier. He had hardly reached the second soldier, when there came a groan

from yet another injured, lying not very far away. The second man motioned him towards the third.

Abu Jahm went to the third man but before he could give him the water to drink, he had expired. Abu Jahm hurried back to the second, but he too had died. He ran back to the place where his cousin was lying, but alas, he had also breathed his last.

Each of the dying soldiers preferred his brother's need to his own. May Allah bless their souls with His mercy, for their sacrifice for others even at the expense of their own lives.

Study Questions

QUESTION 1: Between whom was the Battle of Yarmuk fought?

YOUR RESPONSE: _____

_____

_____

QUESTION 2: Who was the commander of the Muslim Force?

YOUR RESPONSE: _____

_____

QUESTION 3: How many Muslim men took part in this battle?

YOUR RESPONSE: _____

_____

_____

QUESTION 4: What was the number of the enemy?

YOUR RESPONSE:

QUESTION 5: What role did the Muslim women play in this battle?

YOUR RESPONSE:

QUESTION 6: Name some of the Muslim women who took part in the battle.

YOUR RESPONSE:

QUESTION 7: Why is the fourth day of the battle known as the 'Day of the lost eyes'?

YOUR RESPONSE:

QUESTION 8: For whom was Abu Jahm carrying water?

YOUR RESPONSE:

QUESTION 9: Did his cousin drink the water? If not, why?

YOUR RESPONSE:

VICTORIOUS RETURN TO MAKKAH

According to the treaty of Hudaibiyyah, the Arab tribes were given the choice to join either the Makkans or the Muslims. It was also agreed that for ten years the parties would not fight against each other. Under this agreement the tribe of Banu Bakr joined the Makkans while the tribe of Banu Khuzaa'ah entered into an alliance with the Muslims.

It so happened that Banu Bakr, backed by the Makkans, attacked the tribe of Banu Khuzaa'ah and killed many of their men. A deputation of Banu Khuzaa'ah went to the Holy Prophet[saw] and asked for help. As this was a breach of the agreement, the Prophet[saw] promised help and prepared his men to

march upon Makkah. When they came out of Madinah, several other Muslim tribes joined them. After a few days journey, they arrived at Faaraan. The number of Muslims under the command of the Holy Prophet[saw] rose to ten thousand. This was exactly in accordance with the prophecy mentioned in the Old Testament

'My beloved is white and ruddy, the chiefest among ten thousand'. Song of Solomon (5:10)

'And he said, the Lord came from Sinai, and rose up from Seir unto them; he shined forth from mount Paran (Arabic Faaraan) and he came with ten thousand of saints; From his right hand went a fiery law for them'. Deuteronomy (33:2)

As the news of the Muslim force reached Makkah, they sent their leader Abu Sufyaan to find out the number of the Muslim force. Abu Sufyaan came out of Makkah with some of his friends and began travelling towards Madinah. They travelled the whole day and at night they saw an amazing sight. They saw roaring fires at the camp, where the Muslims were staying for the night. There was a fire in front of every tent. Abu Sufyaan was much surprised to see such a large force. He asked his companions 'Has this army dropped from the heavens; I know of no Arab army so large'.

While they were thus wondering, there came a voice from the dark calling Abu Sufyaan. This was Abbaas, who was guarding the camp and was an old friend of Abu Sufyaan. Abbaas persuaded him to accompany him to the Prophet[saw]. The Holy Prophet[saw] told Abbaas to entertain the leader of the Makkans for the night. Early in the morning Abu Sufyaan saw another very unusual sight. He saw them coming out of their tents washing their hands and feet and lining up behind the Holy Prophet[saw]. He was a bit frightened and asked, 'What are they doing?' Abbaas told him that they were only getting ready for morning Prayer.

Abu Sufyaan was much impressed to see how disciplined the Muslims were. In their Prayer, they followed every movement of the Holy Prophet[saw]; standing, bowing, sitting and prostrating.

He said in surprise, 'I have been to great courts. I have seen the court of the Chosroes and the court of the Kaiser, but I have never seen any people as devoted to their leader as the Muslims are to their Prophet'.

Abu Sufyaan realised that there was no chance for them to win against the Muslims. So when the Prayer was over and he was led to the Holy Prophet[saw], he requested him to be kind to the people of Makkah. He was apprehensive that the Muslims might take revenge for the atrocities committed by the Makkans. He, therefore, asked the Prophet[saw], whether the Makkans could have peace, if they did not draw the sword. The Holy Prophet[saw] said, 'Yes, all who stay indoors, will have peace. Whoever takes shelter in Abu Sufyaan's house, will have peace. Whoever enters the Ka'abah will have peace. Those who lay down their arms, will have peace'.

The Prophet[saw] then handed a flag to Abu Ruwaiha, who had entered into a pact of brotherhood with Bilal, and said, 'This is the flag of Bilal, whoever comes under this flag will

have peace'. He told Bilal to march in front of his flag and make an announcement to that effect. Bilal, who had been a slave, and used to be persecuted, humiliated, and disgraced by the Makkans for his belief in Islam, must have felt proud that day, to have the flag of peace in his name.

As the Muslim force marched, column after column towards Makkah, Abu Sufyaan watched them from a cliff. The sight was very impressive. He saw determination on their faces. He saw their devotion to the Holy Prophet[saw]. Here was the man who, seven years ago, had fled from Makkah, for fear of his life, now returned with such force that Makkah was unable to resist him.

Abu Sufyaan rushed back to tell his people about the conditions of peace. The people of Makkah ran for protection, and thus Makkah came into the hands of the Muslims without any blood-shed. There was only one untoward incident which took place on that occasion. The Holy Prophet[saw] had ordered all his followers not to kill anyone unless in self-defence. The part of the town which Khalid entered had not heard the conditions

of peace, so they came out to fight. The result was that twelve or thirteen of the Makkans died.

News of this, was brought quickly to the Holy Prophet[saw], and he immediately issued orders which stopped further bloodshed. In fact, in all the battles which the Holy Prophet[saw] had ever fought in self-defence, he had given clear orders to his followers, not to kill women and children, nor ministers of religion, nor old men, nor those unfit for war. Again, those that laid down their swords were not to be killed. No buildings were to be destroyed. He also forbade cutting down of the fruit trees.

The Holy Prophet[saw], after entering Makkah, made straight for the Ka'abah and performed the circuit of the Holy House seven times. There were 360 idols in the House. The Prophet[saw] smashed them one by one, and as each of them fell, he recited the verse:

> Truth has come and falsehood has vanished away. Falsehood does indeed vanish *fast*. (Holy Quran 17:82)

Thus the Ka'abah was restored to its true purpose, the worship of the one God.

The Prophet[saw] then sent for the leaders of the *Quraish* and asked them what treatment they expected from him. 'The treatment that Joseph accorded to his brethren', they replied. The Holy Prophet[saw] said, 'Then no reproach shall lie on you this day'. This noble treatment by the Holy Prophet[saw] of his bloodthirsty enemies, who had left no stone unturned to kill him and destroy Islam root and branch, stands in history of mankind unparalleled.

Study Questions

QUESTION 1: What were the conditions laid down in the treaty of Hudaibiyyah?

YOUR RESPONSE:

QUESTION 2: Who broke the treaty?

YOUR RESPONSE:

QUESTION 3: Who was the leader of the Makkans? What did he see in the desert at night?

YOUR RESPONSE:

QUESTION 4: What was the prophecy mentioned in the old testament and how did it come true?

YOUR RESPONSE:

QUESTION 5: What were the conditions announced by the Holy Prophet^{saw} for peace?

YOUR RESPONSE: _____

_____

_____

QUESTION 6: What treatment did the Makkans receive from the Holy Prophet^{saw} when Makkah fell to the Muslims?

YOUR RESPONSE: _____

_____

_____

QUESTION 7: Mention some of the Prophet's[saw] precepts about war.

YOUR RESPONSE:

ISLAM ON THE MARCH

The Holy Prophet[saw] of Islam died, but he left behind him:
The Holy Qur'an—a complete guidance for mankind.
His example and sayings.
The faithful Companions—who carried the banner of Islam to the four corners of the world.

The Holy Prophet[saw], himself an unlettered person, had great respect for knowledge. He is reported to have said, 'It is the duty of every Muslim, male or female, to seek knowledge', and that 'The best charity on the part of a Muslim is to acquire knowledge and to impart it to others'.

Thus inspired, Muslims devoted themselves to learning and imparting knowledge with marked success. Throughout the Middle Ages, the Muslim universities and schools ranked best and scholars flocked to them from all parts of the world. They carried out research in almost every field. The doors of these universities were open to all, rich and poor, native and foreign. The poor were encouraged and financed by the State or by the wealthy.

In their zeal for knowledge, the Muslim scholars translated most of the writings of the Greek philosophers into Arabic. It would not be out of place to mention that the Greek works of great importance were preserved only through the efforts of these Muslim scholars. The Muslim artists and painters excelled others in the art of artistic carving, design and specially in the

use of colour. The proof of their skill can still be seen in many parts of the world, for example the Alhambra in Spain, the Blue Mosque in Istanbul, Taj Mahal and other Moghul buildings in India and Pakistan. In these buildings a splendid composition of painted, sculptured or inlaid floral and geometrical designs is displayed.

The Qur'an, being a complete code of life, guided the Muslim scholars of every age, to discover the solution of the problems they faced in their daily lives. It infused in them the spirit to go for discoveries and inventions. In it an appeal is made frequently to ponder over the creation of the vast expanse of the earth and to study the wonderful creation of the heavenly firmament. The Holy Qur'an declared that the heavens with all the celestial bodies and the earth with all its treasures, the deep sea and high mountains, were all created for man's sake.

Inspired by the teachings of the Holy Qur'an, the Muslims began to explore these treasures. They became the pioneers in civilisation and culture, builders of wonderful public

works, organisers of marvellous institutions and founders of a great many sciences and arts. They invented the instruments of astronomy and constructed numerous observatories. With the aid of trigonometry they mapped out the land, charted the seas and plotted the sky. With the invention of the Mariner's compass, they began to roam about the oceans freely. Their frail boats were replaced by larger sailing ships.

Their interest in geography was sparked by these tremendous voyages. They plied the seas as far east as China, explored the coasts of Africa and ranged north to Scandinavia. Some of them travelled overland through Central Asia and north into Russia.

It was the Muslim scholars who introduced the science of Algebra to Europe. In medical science, they had shown great interest. They knew the use of anaesthetics and performed operations on patients. The Muslim physicians of the 11th century introduced the custom of mobile clinics.

A SAMPLE OF ARABIC CALLIGRAPHY

In chemistry they had great success, they discovered many new chemicals e.g.: alcohol, nitric acid, and sulphuric acid. The greatest of all Arab chemists was Jaabir bin Hayyaan (Geber). Some of his discoveries formed the basis of European studies as late as the 18th century. The Muslim scientists of that time applied the knowledge of chemistry to agriculture. They knew the use of fertilizers and crop rotation. Their contribution to metallurgy and ceramics was enormous. Their steel made the name of Toledo and Damascus famous. They also produced the finest kind of leather.

Another great Muslim contribution to the cause of learning was the manufacture of paper, the art of which they learnt from the Chinese perhaps, but perfected it to a great degree. The first paper plant was established in Baghdad towards the end of the 8th century. (A.H.)

They had a great love for literature and books. They established many universities for higher education. Some of them had a worldwide reputation. The universities of Cordova and Toledo in Spain were very popular and attracted scholars from the civilised world of that day.

The Muslim scholars not only produced great works of science and arts of their own, but also translated the ancient works of Greek, Indian and Persian philosophy and medicine into Arabic. Thus the Muslim cities became the centres of learning and knowledge, and the scholars streamed to these centres from everywhere.

As long as the Muslim adhered to the teachings of the Holy Book, they prospered and the whole world looked to them for

guidance. When they ignored this Divine message, their progress halted and gradually their condition became deplorable.

Today, mankind has entered a new era. There has been a rapid advancement of science and technology.

With this rapid change, new problems have arisen, the solution of which can be found in the Holy Qur'an, the fountain of all knowledge. The need of the day is, therefore, to recognise the dynamic character of the guidance of this mighty book. Once, man turns towards God for guidance, He will lead him out of the shadows and the darkness into the light and the path of peace.

Study Questions

QUESTION 1: Mention a saying of the Holy Prophet[saw] which stresses the need of acquiring knowledge.

YOUR RESPONSE: _____

_____

_____

_____

_____

_____

QUESTION 2: Mention some of the Muslim contributions to the development of science and technology.

YOUR RESPONSE: _____

_____

_____

_____

QUESTION 3: What was the cause of the decline of the Muslims?

YOUR RESPONSE: _____

_____

_____

_____

_____

PUBLISHER'S NOTE

Salutations are recited out of respect when mentioning the names of Prophets and holy personages. These salutations have been abbreviated and inserted into the text where applicable. Readers are urged to recite the full salutations for the following abbreviations:

saw — *Sallallaahu 'alaihi wa sallam,* meaning 'May peace and blessings of Allah be upon him', is written after the name of the Holy Prophet Muhammad[saw].

as — *Alaihis-salaam/ Alaihas-salaam,* meaning 'May peace be on him/her', is written after the names of Prophets other than the Holy Prophet Muhammad[saw].

ra — *Radiyallaahu 'anhu/'anhaa/'anhum,* meaning 'May Allah be pleased with him/her/them', is written after the names of the Companions of the Holy Prophet Muhammad[saw] or of the Promised Messiah[as].

rta — *Rahmatullaah 'alaihi/'alaihaa/'alaihim,* meaning 'May Allah shower His mercy upon him/her/them', is written after the names of those deceased pious Muslims who are not Companions of the Holy Prophet Muhammad[saw] or of the Promised Messiah[as].

This book belongs to:

www.ingramcontent.com/pod-product-compliance
Lightning Source LLC
Chambersburg PA
CBHW071614080526
44588CB00010B/1127